M. A. DRAZ obtained his doctorate at the Sorbonne in Paris before ret[illegible]ng to Cairo, where he became Professor of Islamic Studies at Al Az[illegible] University. By the time of his death, in 1958, he had established him[illegible]s one of the world's leading Islamic scholars. His magnum opus, *The* [illegible]*l Word of the Qur'an* (2008), is also published by I.B.Tauris.

‘The subject of the book is so significant, and its author and his approach so impressive, that it is not only essential reading for scholars of the Qur’an, Islam and comparative religions, but is also of great interest to the general reader. Much has been written about the Qur’an in English, mainly by non-Muslim scholars: here we have a work by an outstanding Muslim scholar, who combines his deep knowledge of the Qur’an and Muslim scholarship with an impressive familiarity with French and English works on the subject. This is a book that commends itself to anyone wishing an authoritative, balanced and intellectually engaging introduction to the Qur’an.’

Muhammed Abdel Haleem,
King Fahd Professor of Islamic Studies,
SOAS, London

‘This valuable introduction to the study of the Qur’an by a prominent Azhar scholar provides a rare glimpse of applying modern textual-historical methodology to the study of Muslim scriptures. M. A. Draz understood the challenges of this critical methodology and attempted to respond to some of the persisting questions about the reliability of the Muslim scriptures and its misapprehended message of peace.’

Abdulaziz Sachedina,
Frances Myers Ball Professor of Religious Studies,
University of Virginia

M. A. Draz

Introduction to the Qur'an

I.B.TAURIS
LONDON · NEW YORK

New paperback edition published in 2011 by I.B.Tauris & Co Ltd
6 Salem Road, London W2 4BU
175 Fifth Avenue, New York NY 10010
www.ibtauris.com

Distributed in the United States and Canada Exclusively by Palgrave Macmillan
175 Fifth Avenue, New York NY 10010

First published in hardback in 2000 by I.B.Tauris & Co Ltd

ISBN: 978 1 84885 689 9

A full CIP record for this book is available from the British Library
A full CIP record is available from the Library of Congress

Library of Congress Catalog Card Number: available

Translation by Ayeshah Abdel-Haleem
Printed and bound in Sweden by ScandBook AB
from camera-ready copy supplied by the Centre for Islamic Studies, London

Contents

Foreword

It gives me enormous pleasure to introduce this book finally to readers of English. It has been available to readers of French now for over half a century, and to readers of Arabic for some thirty years. The subject of the book is so significant, and its author and his approach so impressive, that it is not only essential reading for scholars of the Qur'an, Islam and comparative religions, but is also of great interest to the general reader. Much has been written about the Qur'an in English, mainly by non-Muslim scholars; here we have a work by an outstanding Muslim scholar, who combines his deep knowledge of the Qur'an and Muslim scholarship with an impressive familiarity with French and English works on the subject.

The late Professor Muhammad ʿAbd Allāh Draz was born in Egypt in 1894. He came from a family of distinguished scholars in religious studies, and studied at Al-Azhar University, the most ancient and respected of Islamic universities. Draz graduated in 1916, and went on to teach Qur'anic Studies at Al-Azhar for some eight years, commenting on some of the great Islamic scholarly texts, such as the *Muwafaqāt* of Al-Shāṭibī [d 790/1388], one of the classics of Islamic jurisprudence.

He was then sent on a scholarship to prepare for a doctorate at the Sorbonne. In Paris he studied philosophy, the history of religions, psychology and ethics, before embarking on the preparation and writing of two dissertations: this book, under the title *Initiation au Coran*, and the major and monumental *La Morale du Coran*. Both were examined in December 1947, and resulted in Draz being awarded a doctorate with the highest distinction. On his return to Egypt, Draz taught at Al-Azhar and Cairo Universities, producing many distinguished studies in Arabic. He died at a conference in Pakistan in January 1959.

In preparing this book, Draz employed both his great knowledge of the Qur'an and Islamic sources, and his training in Western scholarship at the Sorbonne. His approach, marked by rigorous academic investigation and calm reasoned treatment, succeeds in gaining the respect of the reader. Significantly, he addresses even those orientalists' claims about the Qur'an with which he himself was not in agreement. Perhaps the greatest indication of the soundness of his methods is the applause of his French examiners, who awarded him such a distinguished grade.

The contents page illustrates the fundamental importance of the issues Draz deals with; then, and still now, living issues in Qur'anic scholarship. Muslim scholars find both his study and his approach extremely refreshing. His book stands in a class of its own in its thoroughness, its seriousness in dealing with its subject, and the ideas it raises by both Muslim and non-Muslim scholars. This is a book that commends itself to anyone wishing an authoritative, balanced and intellectually engaging introduction to the Qur'an.

The translation and production of the present work was made possible by a generous contribution from the **Abdallah Al-Zeer Charitable Foundation of Kuwait**, without which this English translation would never have come to light, and to whom the Centre of Islamic Studies wishes to express its profound gratitude.

The next book in the *London Qur'an Studies* series will be Draz's magnum opus, *The Moral World of the Qur'an*.

London, 31 May 2000
Muhammad Abdel Haleem

Preface

Though there are several extremely diverse angles from which one can approach a study of the Qur'an, these will ultimately fall into two main categories: language and ideas. The Qur'an is, simultaneously and on the same level of importance, a work of literature and a book of doctrine.

To study the Qur'an as an artistic, linguistic and rhetorical work presupposes an in-depth knowledge of the Arabic language, in which tongue the text was given. As most educated Europeans (to whom, after all, we principally address ourselves here) are not familiar with this language, we shall not direct the greater part of our efforts on this front, though we will of course touch upon language where this is used to enhance the primary theme or reinforce the implications of the teaching it embodies.

We shall concentrate rather on the treasury of ideas one can discover beneath the Qur'an's literary form. This approach does not require our being Arabs or students of Arabic, yet it nonetheless enables us to undertake a serious and fruitful study of the Qur'an.

Provided that one has a good translation,[1] one can study the Qur'an from any of three angles quite independently of its Arabic form: first of all there is the nature of Qur'anic doctrine, the ensemble of solutions it proposes so as to resolve the two eternal problems of knowledge and action; then there are the means of persuasion the Qur'an employs, in order to establish the truth of this doctrine; and finally there is the manner in which it demonstrates the sacred and Divine character that it attributes to its own message. It is to this quite independent study that we propose to contribute by the present work.

The principal objective of this study is to disengage the Qur'an's moral law from everything which connects it to the rest of the Book. However, before extracting this living cell from the whole organism which is Qur'anic doctrine, we feel it right and useful to present in their indivisible unity the main lines of its doctrinal structure. Thereby we hope to demonstrate the position of the moral element within the integrated framework.

In order to achieve this, we shall first consider the structure that is the Qur'an – rapidly it is true, but with sufficient penetration to discern the generative ideas behind each of its sections, and sufficient breadth to encompass an overall picture of its methods and aims.

Apart from certain indispensable historical guidelines – which we have added at the justified instigation of M. Maurice Patronnier de Gandilla, professor at the Sorbonne – the essential object of the present work is to lay bare in its wholeness the Qur'anic message as the text itself presents it, and not as it has been judged, interpreted or applied across the years.

In treading our path we shall encounter severe judgements passed on the Book which will have to be corrected, and hasty conclusions which will have to be put right, but in principle we shall the leave the words of the Qur'an to provide its own defence and self-justification. Our intervention will consist almost exclusively of coordinating and linking up into a logical sequence the separate pieces that make up this plea of defence, leaving to the reader the task of judging the historical and philosophical validity of the discourse for him- or herself.

The issue at hand is one of studying the Qur'an objectively – insofar as a thinker is able to detach himself from his or her own subjective conditions. To play the role of protagonist does not mean that one is prevented from clothing one's formulations with a personal overtone, an energetic mood, or a persuasive aspect. These should be seen as the reflection which the original projects onto its mirror, and not an essentially novel accretion of our particular manner of thinking.

It is necessary to say that, in divesting the Qur'anic idea of its clothing, and thus disengaging it from its local framework so as to make it accessible to those unfamiliar with the Arabic language, we are doing no more than helping to reveal its true purpose. Appealing constantly to reason, common sense and the more generous human sentiments, the Qur'an addresses itself in effect to all mankind, regardless of national roots or ethnic origins.

The Qur'an is a universal teaching which aims to purify customs, to throw light on and reconcile beliefs, to cause racial barriers and national chauvinism to fall, and to replace the law of brute strength with that of truth and justice. In addition to its contribution to world philosophy, however, it also serves as a precious source of succour for those who study it during this frenetic period of domination and destruction.

Paris, 21 February 1947
M.D.

Part One
Background History

Before we engage in a methodical analysis of the sacred Book of Islam, we should call to mind the conditions under which it appeared, and the stages it has undergone before reaching us today.

We shall first give some key dates in the early life of the Prophet, since his history is linked inseparably with that of the Qur'an. Whatever the nature of the criteria we bring to bear upon the origin, Divine or human, of the Qur'an, there is no doubt that historically speaking the Qur'an is a Muhammadan phenomenon. This is irrespective of whether, as the sceptics say, the Prophet drew it from within himself or from the surrounding ambience of knowledge at this time, or whether, as the Qur'an affirms on many occasions, he received it in textual form at the dictation of a celestial messenger serving as intermediary between God and Muhammad.

> *For surely he revealed it to thy heart by Allah's command, verifying that which is before it and a guidance and glad tidings for the believers.*
>
> 2:97

Since we, with our limited experience and knowledge, could never aspire to such a superhuman source, we may say definitively that it is from Muhammad that we obtain this text, be it as the author himself or as the unique intermediary of its reproduction and transmission to all humanity.

1
The Early Life of the Prophet

Given such a close liaison between the Messenger and his message, and since our work is destined principally for milieux barely familiar with the story of the Arab Prophet, we shall commence by giving a concise portrait of Muhammad from his childhood up to the time when he was invested with his world mission.

Who, then, was this man? He belonged to a greatly illustrious family from Mecca, the Hashemite branch of the tribe of Quraysh, known for its religious, rather than political, nobility. Tradition has it that he is descended from Ismāʿīl, son of Abraham, through 21 named generations as far back as ʿAdnān, then through several generations whose precise number and names are engulfed in obscurity and uncertainty.[1]

According to the unanimous opinion of his biographers, Muhammad was born on a Monday in the second week of the lunar month Rabīʿ al-Awwal,[2] in the Year of the Elephant. This was the year of the invasion of the Hejaz, unsuccessfully undertaken by Abraha, then vice-roy of Yemen, under the domination of the Byzantines, with an army containing the largest elephant in the Abyssinian kingdom. The most accredited scholars say that this event corresponds with the year 53 before the Hijra, that is, the year 571 AD.

Muhammad was born an orphan, his father ʿAbd Allāh having died seven months before his birth:

Did He not find thee an orphan and give (thee) shelter?

93:6

Following a custom held sacrosanct by the notables of the city, whereby their new-born babies were reared in the salubrious air of the country, the child was consigned to the care of a Bedouin wet-nurse, Ḥalīma, of the tribe of Banī Saᶜd, until he reached the age of four. His mother Amīna then undertook his education, helped by an Abyssinian housekeeper, Umm Ayman.

Unhappily, he was not to benefit long from such loving maternal care. Losing his mother at the age of six, the orphan was then taken into the guardianship of his grandfather, ᶜAbd al-Muṭṭalib, who showed the boy special affection and predicted a great future for him. Hardly had he reached the age of eight, however, than he lost his grandfather too. From now on he received the protection of his uncle ᶜAbd Manāf, surnamed Abū Ṭālib.

Although already burdened with a very large family, and finding his situation far from easy, Abū Ṭālib reserved a sincere paternal love for his nephew, and was aware that a relative prosperity reigned in his house from the time that the young boy entered it. He held great store by having Muhammad by his side at all times, and, in a reciprocal attachment, the young man did not wish any the more to be separated from his uncle. Thus we find Muhammad (then aged 12) accompanying his uncle on a trading trip to Syria in 582.

Linked to this journey is the famous account of Muhammad's first contact with religion, in the person of a Christian monk at Boṣra (then in Syria), called Baḥīrā. The tradition says that this sage, having noticed in the march of the caravan certain signs recounted in the sacred texts, invited the party to dine with him. He set about examining the faces of the travellers, so as to compare their appearance with the documents in his possession, but they did not tally. Then, after questioning our youth, who arrived later at the scene, Baḥīrā approached Abū Ṭālib and said to him: 'This young man will be called upon to play a great role in the world. Tell him to return to your country as soon as possible; but watch over him always and beware especially of the Jews, who could do him evil if they knew what I know about him.'[3]

There is little detail to tell about Muhammad's life between this event and his marriage. We know that he spent his youth in a state bordering on poverty, as the Qur'an describes:

And find thee in want, so He enriched thee?

93:8

The tradition explains the Prophet's situation as follows: since his father died young while his grandfather was still alive, the only inheritance Muhammad received on the death of his mother was a black slave, a herd of sheep and five camels. His most frequent occupation during this period seems to have been that of shepherd – a function performed, he was later to say, by the earlier prophets, such as Moses, David and others.

Muhammad stood out from other adolescents on account of his refined manners, the most evident of which was his extreme modesty. He distanced himself from the easy pleasures of most young people, and was absolutely chaste. He inspired a lively interest in all those with whom he felt in harmony, and the confidence he engendered in the hearts of his companions merited the surname they gave him: al-Amīn (the trustworthy). Such solid qualities as these do not generally pass unnoticed, and thus we see Muhammad, while still a young man (aged 20), called upon to sit beside the most venerable chiefs of the tribes in the Fuḍūl confederation.[4]

As well as marking a time of prosperity for him, Muhammad's marriage at the age of 25 revealed in him other, no less excellent, qualities. Charged with a business mission by his wife Khadīja, a virtuous, rich and noble widow of middle age, he acquitted himself with intelligence and honesty, confirming for her the name he had already earned from his comrades. Indeed, despite the material differences separating the two, it was she who made overtures towards him concerning marriage, to which he agreed, notwithstanding the age difference between them.

For a quarter of a century Khadīja remained Muhammad's only wife. Death alone was able to separate them, leaving her faithful remembrance to arouse the naive jealousy of his later household. She presented him with two boys, al-Qāsim and ʿAbd Allāh, both of whom died when they were still young,[5] and four daughters, Zaynab, Ruqayya, Umm Kulthūm and Fāṭima, all of whom embraced Islam. The latter was to become the wife of ʿAlī, the fourth caliph; the two next youngest were successively to marry ʿUthmān, the third caliph. As for the eldest, Zaynab, before the time of Islam's advent, she married one of her maternal cousins, Abū 'l-ʿĀs, who later converted. She died two years before her father, leaving a daughter, Umāma, who married ʿAlī after Fāṭima's death.

An excellent father and faithful spouse, Muhammad showed deep tenderness towards his children and grandchildren. He would walk several miles just to see them and embrace them when they stayed in the care of their wet-nurses; he would allow them to cling to his neck during prayer; and he would interrupt his preaching in order to bid them welcome and place them beside him on his chair. His interchanges with the Bedouin of Tamīm are well known on the subject of paternal feelings.[6]

Despite his having become wealthy through marriage, Muhammad remained simple and frugal, only taking advantage of his easy circumstances in order to generate bounty around him. Thus, in order to acquit himself of the debt of gratitude he owed to the uncle who had looked after him during his childhood, he took it upon himself to aid him in the education of his youngest son, ʿAlī, to whom he was later to give Fāṭima, the youngest of his daughters.

The most prominent event between his marriage and his calling to prophethood took place when Muhammad was 35 years old, on the occasion of the renovation of the Kaʿba. This monument may be considered to have been the national temple of Arabia, since all of the Arab tribes, despite the diversity of their cults, shrouded it in the most profound veneration. They all laid great importance upon procuring for themselves the honour of participating in its reconstruction and, so as to satisfy all possible claims, it was arranged by a form of division of labour that all would be given work.

One day those taking part in the reconstruction found themselves faced with a job they could not share equally among themselves: the putting in place of the famous Black Stone. No one wanted to cede the right to make it his responsibility, nor could anyone ward off an imminent conflict. Before running to take up arms, however, one last conference was held.

It was decided to resort to the arbitration of the first person to enter the sacred precinct through the Banī Shayba gate, and, as chance would have it, this person was Muhammad. As soon as they saw him enter, they shouted: 'al-Amīn, al-Amīn!' They were not to be disappointed in their expectation of an equitable solution.

With the presence of mind and impartiality to which Muhammad's life had always given evidence, he laid out his cloak on the earth, placed the Black Stone in the middle, and asked the head chiefs of each tribe to take an edge of the cloak and lift it simultaneously to the prescribed height. Arriving thus at the location which the Stone was to occupy, he then took it himself and put it in place with his own hands. Unanimous satisfaction was complete, and immediate peace was re-established.

By now, Muhammad was physically, intellectually and morally complete, and his character thus formed would remain with him to the end of his life. Of a stature slightly above the average, he was solidly built, with a wide chest and shoulders, a large head and a wide forehead. He had a large mouth and white teeth slightly separate from each another, an abundant beard, black wavy hair which fell in curls around his eyes, white skin with a pink tinge, black eyes and bloodshot corneas. His gait was both lithe and imposing, as if he were in the middle of descending a slope, and he wore simple clothes that were clean and well-cared for.

He was always serene and had a rare sobriety, without, however, denying himself the enjoyment of good things when the occasion presented itself. He showed effortless endurance under difficulty and fatigue; he was usually collected and spoke little, this economy of speech neither meaning that he did not enjoy conversation nor that he was not sensitive to innocent playfulness.

Once he had become the chief and sole leader of the state, Muhammad was tempted neither by riches nor the goods of this world. He deliberately brushed aside all kinds of luxury in all spheres, both for himself and for his family. The most formal indication of this attitude may be seen in his anger at those in his family who wanted the ostentatious glitter of this life:

> *O Prophet, say to thy wives: If you desire this world's life and its adornment, come, I will give you a provision and allow you to depart a goodly departing. But if you desire Allāh and His Messenger and the abode of the Hereafter, then surely Allāh has prepared for the doers of good among you a mighty reward.*
>
> 33:28-9

Eventually, the few possessions Muhammad owned were not even destined to be inherited by his relatives, but were distributed in their entirety to the poor after his death.

It is in social matters above all that we see Muhammad at his most admirable. Endowed with an exemplary gentleness and a fastidiousness which never left him, not even when at the height of his power, he was never curt in conversation – regardless of with whom he was speaking – and never showed impatience. He was never the first to withdraw his hand from his interlocutor, and showed firmness and impartiality in the dispensation of justice in the community. He was very indulgent in anything connected with personal rights; one of his servants, Anas bin Mālik, affirms that during the ten years of his service he was never scolded by his master, nor even questioned about his motives for doing one thing rather than another.

Although he lived at peace with the world, and knew how to win affection and admiration in all circles, it was not long before Muhammad provoked animosity against himself and against those people who used to hold him so dear. He was by now nearing 40, and was on the eve of a decisive event which would stamp a new orientation upon his conduct, an event which in the wider view would constitute a veritable turning point in history.

The first indication of his vocation as a prophet, according to his own account given to ʿĀ'isha, consisted in the fact that everything he saw in his dreams would then take place by the following evening, 'with a clarity resembling that of daylight.' Following this, he experienced a certain inclination for solitude. As a place of retreat his choice fell upon Mount Ḥirā', or Jabal al-Nūr (mountain of light) to the north of Mecca. There, far from the impious and corrupt environment of the town, and far too from all worldly preoccupations, he liked to retire into a cave overlooking the venerated temple of the Kaʿba and the firmament which spread to infinity behind it.[7]

It was on one such night, according to Ibn Saʿd on the 17th of Ramaḍān to be exact (February 610 AD), that Muhammad entered into contact for the first time with the beyond. In this absolute calm, he had his first experience of the phenomenon of genuine revelation.

The manner in which this happened is described by Muhammad himself in the form of a dialogue taking place between himself and Gabriel, the disciple and his preceptor.

'Read!' said the angel. 'I am not of those who knows how to read,' replied Muhammad, astonished. 'Read!' repeated Gabriel, at the same time squeezing him almost unbearably. 'What should I read?' Muhammad asked. The same order to read was then reiterated with even greater pressure, as though to awaken his attention to its extreme limits, and to inculcate in his soul the full seriousness of the superhuman task to be placed upon him. 'How can I read?' repeated our terrified recluse. And so the angel recited to him:[8]

> *Read in the name of thy Lord who creates – creates man from a clot, read, and thy Lord is most generous, who taught by the pen, taught man what he knew not.*
>
> 96:1-5

These words were fixed indelibly in Muhammad's memory; he repeated them to himself, and then the angel disappeared. But hardly had he emerged from the cave to return home, than he heard a voice calling to him. He raised his head, and there was an angel, filling the sky beyond the horizon and declaring: 'O Muhammad! In truth, you are the Messenger of God, and I, I am Gabriel.' It was not possible for him to avert his gaze, to move forward or to retreat; there was no part of the sky in which he could not see the angel. This lasted a certain time, and then he saw no more.

Muhammad was filled with awe at such an unprecedented visual and auditory experience. No doubt, for a moment, it aroused some doubt in him as to the identity of the voice that had revealed these things. He held a fear of having been the victim of a diabolic hallucination – he who detested nothing more than the methods of sorcerers and diviners, and who would dread to be classed as one of their ilk. Perhaps also, in his eyes, the bodily suffering he experienced as a result of this encounter resembled the death throes, and therefore he believed that he was no longer alive. Feeling a mixture of moral and physical disturbance, he returned directly home and, agitated by a sort of cold fever, asked to be wrapped in heavy coverings in order that his terror might be dissipated.

Divulging the incident to Khadīja later, Muhammad gave voice to his fear and perplexity. His devoted companion reassured him with all her might, using her wisest and most comforting words.

'No,' she said to him, 'Do not afflict yourself. On the contrary, this is good news, which should cause you to rejoice. Surely God would not wish to inflict evil upon you, nor to cover you with shame, for you have never done anything bad. You always tell the truth; you maintain all the bonds which bind those near to you in an excellent way; you help the weak; you give money to those who need it; you show hospitality to all your guests; and you give your help to all those who suffer for a just cause.'

However, being unable to give a positive or certain explanation of the nature of the event, Khadīja felt the need to seek the opinion of some competent authority. So she decided to go with Muhammad to consult such a one: her cousin, Waraqa bin Nawfal, an old man converted to Christianity. Waraqa was well-versed in Hebrew and familiar with the holy Books, though he was by now quite blind.

'If the account you give is precise,' said Waraqa, 'then this can be none other than the Nāmūs,[9] which God revealed to Moses. This means that Muhammad will be the Messenger of God to this nation. Would that I could live to the day when your compatriots will expel you from your country!'

'What?' cried Muhammad. 'They will expel me?'

'But assuredly,' replied Waraqa. 'Never has it been that a man brings what you bring without becoming the object of hostilities and persecutions. But if God prolongs my days until that time, and if I possess enough energy, I will lend you the strongest support in this battle.'

Waraqa did not live that long, however. And though his comforting words had been able to throw some gleam of hope onto Muhammad's anxious soul, despite the Prophet's hunger for knowledge, evidence and certainty, the hope in this truly positive spirit was still not so very strong, and in the event did not last long. For what could be more natural, if this promised knowledge had been announced by the voice of truth, than to wait and see from one day to the next whether this promise would be fulfilled?

And so Muhammad often returned to seek out a second lesson, in the same place in which he had received his first. He put himself into the same conditions as before; he roved around the mountain, turning his gaze in all directions. And the days passed, the weeks flew by, months succeeded months, a year ended and another began and, according to al-Shaʿbī, then a third, and yet nothing more happened. The only exception is that, each time he found himself on the edge of the abyss of despair, he would see and hear: 'O, Muhammad! You are, in truth, the Messenger of God and I, I am Gabriel.' These words would calm him somewhat, but then he would relapse into sadness and anguish, anxiously awaiting any substantial revelation.

Some said: 'Surely this is nothing more than madness!' Others surmised that a priceless celestial offering had indeed been made, but that, due to his fragile stamina, Muhammad had shown himself incapacitated and, consequently, unworthy of Divine concern. Two short Qur'anic revelations reassured the Prophet himself against these fears, though they did not go on to provide the teaching he so much hoped for:

> *By the grace of thy Lord thou art not mad.*
>
> 68:2

> *Thy Lord has not forsaken thee, nor is He displeased.*
>
> 93:3

Muhammad made it his duty to stay awake throughout a large part of the night, waiting for the promised 'words of great gravity':

> *O thou covering thyself up! Rise to pray by night except a little, half of it, or lessen it a little, or add to it, and recite the Qur'ān in a leisurely manner. Surely We shall charge thee with a weighty word. The rising by night is surely the firmest way to tread and most effective in speech. Truly thou hast by day prolonged occupation.*
>
> 73:1-7

Furthermore, since the occurrence of the first revelation, he had adopted the habit of retiring to Mount Ḥirā' at the same period each year, that is to say in the month of Ramaḍān.

At last, in his 43rd lunar year, the Prophet had just completed his retreat and descended the slope in the direction of the town, when he heard someone call to him. He looked to the right, then to the left, then behind him – and saw nothing. Then, raising his eyes to the sky, he recognized the angel he had seen at Ḥirā'. The suddenness of the apparition and the majestic immensity of the celestial being struck him so forcibly that his legs were unable to support him. Trembling with fear (and perhaps also from the January cold), he returned to Khadīja to ask her for the same ministrations as on the first occasion.

This time, however, the honourable visitor appeared before him once more, at his home, and conveyed to him the decree whereby he was invested with his second role:

> *O thou who wrappest thyself up, arise and warn.*
>
> 74:1-2

Thus, Muhammad received not only a Divine teaching, but also a command to transmit this message to the people. His role as Messenger was from now on connected to that of Preacher of God's word.

Between the two investitures described above, Muhammad experienced long intervals between his inspirations. Moreover, these were prone to abruptness of appearance and disappearance, and tended to be fairly insubstantial. From the time of his vocation to preach, however, the Prophet received his revelations if not regularly, or even frequently, at least with a certain continuity and without such sudden breaks.

The year 612 was the true point of departure in the career of the Messenger of Islam, a career which the date of the Hijra comes to divide into two almost equal parts:[10] ten years in Mecca, the town where he was born, and ten more at Medina, his later residence. It was here that he was to die, on 12 or 13 Rabīʿ al-Awwal in the eleventh year of the Hijra (7 or 8 June 632 AD), aged exactly 63 lunar years, or slightly more than 61 solar years.[11]

Without doubt, it would be very interesting to follow Muhammad in his indefatigable evangelizing activity during these two decades. After all, they brought about one of the greatest civilizing revolutions humanity has ever known. But since the principal object of this work is the analysis of the Qur'anic system itself, having brought the study of Muhammad's life to the point where the union between the message and the Messenger has begun to be effected, we may now move on to consider the Work he has left to us. In the following chapter, we shall describe the manner in which the work was composed, ordered, conserved and transmitted across history.

2
The Composition of the Revealed Text

Today the Qur'an is presented as one volume, most commonly arranged over about 500 pages of 15 lines each, and divided into 114 *sūras* (chapters) of unequal length. After the *Fātiḥa* (opening), which consists of five short lines, the *sūras* are in general arranged in order of descending length,[1] with the longest at the beginning,[2] those of medium length in the middle, and the shortest (some of which are only one line long) at the end. Diacritical signs, vocalization, orthographic and punctuation marks are all included, so as to guide the reader in its correct pronunciation and pauses.

Yet the Qur'an would not have looked like this during the time of the Prophet: while the text itself remains rigorously as it was given under his dictation, its appearance in the written form has changed considerably. In the beginning, it was not what one might call a volume, for, as we have already demonstrated by the few examples given above, the Qur'an appeared piece by piece, with each piece being of shorter or longer length, varying from an entire *sūra* to a single verse, or sometimes even part of a verse. As each fragment inspired in the Prophet was recited by him, it would be learned by his listeners and spread further to those who had not heard it directly from his lips.

Muhammad's followers waited fervently for each fragment, and desired to have it imparted to them as and when it emerged. Indeed, even the enemies of the Prophet, far from being indifferent to his Qur'an, tried often to listen to its recitation, either to find a weak point in it which might lead them to challenge or attack him, or to assuage their passionate appetite for literature. Imagine, then, the interest it must have inspired in its adherents! For them, the Qur'an was food for the spirit, a rule of conduct, a text for prayer, an instrument for preaching; it was their hymn and their history, their fundamental law and code for all circumstances in life.

But the sacred text is not only a 'recitation' (*qur'ān*), an assemblage of oral recitations destined solely to be conserved in the memory, it is also a *kitāb*, a 'scripture' or 'book', with the two aspects corroborating and controlling each other mutually. Each fragment inspired in the Prophet and recited by him was immediately put down in writing on anything the scribes could lay their hands on: leaves, planks, pieces of parchment, leather, flat stones, shoulder-blades and so on.

The most trustworthy scholars describe up to 29 people who were called upon by the Prophet to fulfill the role of secretary. The most well-known are the first five caliphs (Abū Bakr, ʿUmar, ʿUthmān, ʿAlī, Muʿāwiya) plus al-Zubayr bin al-ʿAwwām, Saʿīd bin al-ʿĀṣ, ʿAmr bin al-ʿĀṣ, Ubayy bin Kaʿb and Zayd bin Thābit, with Muʿāwiya and Zayd bin Thābit being the most prolific. But, over and above these few who were unofficially given this office in Mecca, from the very outset and even in the midst of persecutions, the individual faithful were constantly recording fragments of the revealed text in personal manuscripts for private use.

A story handed down to us tells us that the conversion of ʿUmar was due to his reading a leaf of just such writing which he found on his sister, and which bore the first verses of the 20th *sūra*:

> *Tā hā. We have not revealed the Qur'ān to thee that thou mayest be unsuccessful; but it is a reminder to him who fears: a revelation from Him Who created the earth and the high heavens. The Beneficent is established on the Throne of Power. To Him belongs whatever is in the heavens and whatever is in the earth and whatever is between them and whatever is beneath the soil. And surely if thou utter the saying aloud, surely He knows the secret, and what is yet more hidden. Allāh – there is no God but He. His are the most beautiful names.*
>
> 20:1-8

At this stage, these written documents were not meant to form a crude version of a homogeneously ordered and numbered collection: the Prophet himself did not own one written fragment and not one person around him had in his possession a complete collection of what had so far been revealed. Scattered thus amongst the faithful, it was not possible that they should find a definitive arrangement in the communal memory until towards the end of the Prophet's life.

Yet, from quite early on it was easy for the faithful to see that these revealed fragments were not destined to remain entirely isolated, but neither should they take their place one after the other in the chronological order of their revelation. It came about that several groups of passages were developing in distinct definition from each other. Little by little, with the addition of other verses, these began to constitute independent wholes. These would then be linked together, added to here or intercalated there, all on the express indications of the Prophet, which he himself affirmed to be in conformity with the orders of the celestial spirit.

Due to the continuous nature of this process of construction, the faithful were obliged to await the completion of the whole work before the individual strands could be pulled into one body. Yet, despite this lack of a sequential order in the written fragments at this stage, each oral passage at every stage of the developing revelation knew its destined place within the entire *sūra* concerned.[3] It was the same for the prayer, as it was also for the teaching, preaching and other recitations.

Thus, in the lifetime of the Prophet, several hundred of the Companions, known as 'the carriers of the Qur'an', were already specialized in reciting the Book and knew each *sūra* in its given form, be it provisional or definitive. We have Ibn Mas'ūd, for example, priding himself on having learned more than 70 *sūra*s from the lips of the Prophet. In turn, the Prophet affirms that every year in the month of Ramaḍān he made a general revision of the text by reciting everything thus far revealed through Gabriel; and that in the last year the Divine Messenger twice checked through the Qur'an with him, which presaged to him his approaching end.

Barely a year had passed after the Prophet's death before the faithful began to assemble these scattered documents and try to make them into a manageable, easy-to-consult collection, with the fragments within each chapter following their appointed sequence, as they had been learned by memory, but the overall arrangement remaining unfixed. The impetus for this came from 'Umar, who suggested the idea to Abū Bakr after hundreds of Muslims, including 70 'carriers of the Qur'an', were killed at the battle of Yamāma against the false prophet, Musaylima. Fearing a progressive diminution in the number of readers by further wars, a collection of these Qur'anic fragments would safeguard the totality of the written sources in a state which could be consulted in times of need. It would also serve to sanction a unified form of this document on the authority of its existing readers and all the Companions, who each knew a smaller or greater amount by heart.[4]

The task was entrusted to Zayd bin Thābit. Aware of the heavy responsibility involved in such an enterprise, Zayd hesitated at first to accept it. But Abū Bakr insisted: 'You are an intelligent man. We do not have the slightest suspicion concerning your honesty, since you wrote the revelations at the dictation of the Prophet. Take it upon yourself, therefore, to gather together the Qur'an.'[5] Another factor contributing towards the choice of

Zayd seems to have been that, in addition to being a scribe and a carrier, he had been present at the final recitation, during which the Prophet had presented the ensembled Qur'an.[6]

A working methodology was established and rigorously applied: no writing was to be accepted unless certified by two witnesses as having been put down, not from memory, but at the very dictation of the Prophet, and as being part of the text as given in its final state. According to al-Layth bin Saʿd, the exigence of two witnesses meant that even a passage contributed by ʿUmar concerning the punishment of adulterers by stoning was excluded, since ʿUmar had been the sole witness.[7]

Having completed this task with all of these precautions followed, Zayd placed his recension in the hands of Abū Bakr, who kept it with him during his caliphate. Before his death, the first caliph entrusted it to ʿUmar, whom he had designated as his successor. ʿUmar, in turn, rendered it in his last moments into the protection of his daughter, Ḥafṣa, a widow of the Prophet, since the third caliph had not been elected at that time.

This first official recension (which one can imagine as taking the form of a dossier of ordered sheets in an unbound pile) differed from other existing entire or partial copies because of the absolute rigour exercised at its collation, and because of its exclusion of all that was not part of the text in its final recited form. For example, Ibn Masʿūd or Ubayy bin Kaʿb, when compiling their recensions, sometimes wrote from memory, putting in variants belonging to an earlier period, or permitting themselves to mark small explanatory notes,[8] or certain prayer formulas not included in the text,[9] either in the margin or between the lines of their copies, often in a different colour. The official recension, by contrast, may be seen to be purified even of the titles of its chapters.

In spite of the enormous value attached to such a document, and the laudable care that had been taken in establishing it, the official recension maintained a more or less private character during the years that it remained preciously guarded with the first two caliphs. Indeed, it did not acquire its universal authority until the day it was published, during the rule of ʿUthmān, the third caliph.

During the battles of Armenia and Azerbaijan, dispute arose when the armies of Syria and Iraq realized that there were differences in wording on each side. The Syrians followed the reading of their fellow citizen, Ubayy, while the Iraqis followed that of theirs, Ibn Masʿūd, with the one side saying to the other: 'What we have learned is better than what you have learned.' Frightened by this spectacle, Ḥudhayfa bin al-Yamān went to the Caliph ʿUthmān, and urgently requested him to put an end to 'such disputes, which could end in divisions similar to those of the Jews and the Christians on the question of their Books'.

ʿUthmān accordingly instituted a committee of four copyists, being the same Zayd of Medina and three others from Mecca: ʿAbd Allāh bin al-Zubayr, Saʿīd bin al-Āṣ and ʿAbd al-Raḥmān bin al-Ḥārith bin Hishām. Charging them with copying the original, still under Ḥafṣa's care, into as many copies as there were principal towns in the Muslim empire,[10] he specified: 'If there is any disagreement between you on the spelling of any word,[11] write it according to the Qurayshī dialect, for it was in this dialect that the Qur'an was (originally) given.' The work was thus completed in perfect accordance with the original, which was then returned to Ḥafṣa, and the copies bound and distributed as the standard model of the Qur'an. Any variations showing deviations from this were rendered void.

Certain Shīʿites suspected ʿUthmān of having distorted the text of the Qur'an, or more precisely, of having omitted parts referring to ʿAlī. If this fact were true, the 'carriers of the Qur'an', who were still very numerous at the time when it was published, would have been able to verify this by comparing it with what they knew by heart. But even Ibn Masʿūd, who had more than one reason to be displeased with the political situation, recognized the accuracy of the work no less than others, and predicted that at 'a later time there will be many who read the Qur'an, but few who are wise; when the letters of the Qur'an will be respected, but the application of its commandments neglected'.[12] Even given the zeal of the first Muslims, who were more ardent than their successors towards the word of God, it is inconceivable to attribute to a mere spirit of conformity the fact that the recension of ʿUthmān was accepted by everyone without contradiction. Nöldeke concludes that one should see in this the best proof that the text 'was as complete and faithful as one could make it'.[13]

Whatever the case may be, this edition has been the only one in force in the Muslim world for 13 centuries, including among the Shīʿites. Consider the profession of faith of the Imāmites (the most important sect within Shīʿism), as it is found in the work of Abu Jaʿfar of Qum: 'Our belief concerning the amount of the Qur'an, which God the Most High revealed to His Prophet Muhammad (may peace and blessing be upon him and his family), is that it consists of what has been preserved up to now between two covers for the use of men, and nothing more. The number of *sūra*s recognized by most Muslims is 114, but according to us *sūra*s 93 and 94 form one *sūra* and *sūra*s 105 and 106 form another; it is the same with *sūra*s eight and nine. He who ascribes to us the belief that the Qur'an is more than this is a liar.'[14]

Leblois has also been able to affirm: 'The Qur'an is today the only sacred Book which does not present notable variants.'[15] Muir proclaimed the same before him: 'The recension of ʿUthmān has passed from hand to hand to us without alteration. It has been so scrupulously conserved that there are no serious variants (and one could even say that there are none) in the innumerable copies of the Qur'an which circulate within the vast domain of Islam ... There has never been anything other than one Qur'an for every faction, however implacable; and this unanimous usage of the same scripture accepted by all up to the present day is one of the unchallengeable proofs of the trustworthiness of the text which we possess, and which goes right back to the unfortunate caliph [ʿUthmān, who was assassinated].'[16]

While demonstrating an unimpeachable impartiality in historical matters, these judgements nevertheless call for a twofold correction, for they err both by default and by excess. Thus, they are wrong to imply that the source of the Qur'anic text we possess goes back only as far as the third caliph, ʿUthmān, for as we have already seen he did no more than make public the manuscript brought together under Abū Bakr. More than this, we have seen how this same original was nothing other than the integral reproduction, according to the order of recital (an order which should not be confused with that of the order of its revelation) of the text as taken down at the dictation of the Prophet himself.

Furthermore, it is going too far to categorically state that these editions, although repeating each other graphically, do not contain any variant in pronunciation. Even those with only the slightest knowledge of Arabic writing will know that, though long vowels have nearly always been represented within the body of Arabic words, this has never been so with short vowels, nor with certain medial vowels; in addition, several groups of letters not only resemble each other, but are identical in their manner of writing, the one being only distinguishable from the other by diacritical points. In this way, (n) can be read as (t), (b) or (y), according to whether one or two dots are placed above or below it. Yet, neither during the lifetime of the Prophet nor at the time of the first three caliphs were such points used.

Thus, while common sense sufficed in some cases to guess the precise pronunciation of a word, most often this could not be certain unless indicated orally. To complicate matters, tradition tells us that the Prophet himself did not always keep to one version in his teaching. From the same word (or rather from the same radical) it was not unusual for him to give several instructions, all good and meaningful. Thus a word could be read *mālik* (master, owner) or *malik* (king); in the same way a word could be read *fatabayyanū* (inform yourselves) or *fatathabbatū* (act with circumspection), and traditionally these different readings are equally acceptable.

Among the Companions, from the very beginning, there grew different forms of reading, often mutually unknown to each other. Al-Bukhārī reports that one day ʿUmar heard Hishām bin Ḥakīm bin Ḥizām reciting *sūra* 25 in a way different to that which he had himself learned from the Prophet, and became very angry. Indeed, he found it difficult to control his fury whilst

Hishām was saying his prayers and, as soon as Hishām had finished, seized him by the throat and asked him from whom he had learned this manner of saying the *sūra*.

'From the lips of the Prophet,' Hishām replied. 'You are lying,' said ʿUmar, 'for the Prophet taught it to me differently,' and he led him to Muhammad. The Prophet then ordered Hishām to recite, and approved his reading, saying that the *sūra* had indeed been thus revealed. Then he did the same with ʿUmar and added: 'In truth, the Qur'an is revealed in seven readings, or variants;[17] recite the one which is the easiest among them.' Al-Ṭabarī tells us that Ubayy bin Kaʿb was equally shocked by a difference in reading concerning *sūra* 16, and that he, too, had recourse to the arbitration of the Prophet, who approved both readings.

Was ʿUthmān, then, more exacting than his Master in forbidding readings which the latter had allowed? It does not seem so to us, for ʿUthmān too did not mean to abolish every nuance of pronunciation. Just like those preceding it, his edition was made up of skeleton words, susceptible to different readings. In every case where the orthography of the words could not be resolved by one possible reading, ʿUthmān took great pains to render explicit the different readings traditionally allowed. Thus we see the word *musayṭir* written with a *sīn* topped by a *ṣād*, or with a *ṣād* topped by a *sīn*, while we find *sāraʿū* in one of the master copies, *wa-sāraʿū* in another; similarly *bi-mā tashtahī* and *bi-mā tashtahīhi*; *sayaqūlūna Allāh* and *sayaqūlūna li-llāh*.

The publication of the Qur'anic text under the supervision of ʿUthmān had, in our view, a double purpose. First, it sought to legitimize and protect all the different readings which had a prophetic origin communally recognized, in order to prevent impious disputes about them. As ʿUthmān himself explained: 'To say that such a reading is better than such another almost amounts to unbelief.'[18] Second, it sought to exclude everything that did not show an absolute identity with the original, so as to 'ward off' any possible serious rift between Muslims, or any eventual alteration of the text by the insertion of certain variants. These may have been the subjects of discussion, or the various explanations of individuals, who might have added them in good faith to their copies.

On the other hand, we should not be under the misapprehension that this ʿUthmānī edition, and even less its prototype, contains all the variants probably taught by the Prophet under the heading *Sabʿat Aḥruf*, or 'seven ways of reading'. For although the edition conserved those readings which witnesses accepted as having been incorporated in the text in its definitive stage, it at the same time excluded any form transmitted by individuals who could not provide such a guarantee.[19] From the very beginning, the thousands of Companions were united on the practicality of this basic principle.[20]

The criteria for exclusion of a reading from the written document do not appear to have carried into the sphere of the spoken text: those who affirmed that the Prophet had read a text in a certain way were at liberty to follow their particular versions under their own moral responsibility, but not to attempt to make that version authoritative for the community at large. This fair and reasonable approach is demonstrated by ʿUthmān's response to the political insurgents: 'As to the Qur'an, I have only forbidden readings to you on account of my fear of dispute, but you can read what you wish as you follow the letters.'[21] Also the *fatwā* of Imām Mālik, where he makes it permissible to recite *fa'mḍū* according to the reading of ʿUmar, instead of *fa'sʿaw* (62:9).[22] Ibn ʿAbd al-Barr specifies that, 'during the obligatory prayers,' non-ʿUthmānī readings are not a sure enough Qur'an to do their duty.[23]

It can be seen, then, that outside its ritual recitation and incorporation in the codex, all other usage stays entirely open. Islamic scholarship of every age has not ceased to be interested in the study of these particular readings. It is this double point which Dr Arthur Jeffrey, editor of *Kitāb al-Maṣṣāḥif*, has not rightly understood. On the one hand 'this investigation' is not 'in its infancy in the Muslim world', as he supposes.[24] We need look no further than the number of Arabic works which Jeffrey himself utilizes on this subject; not only special treatises on orthography, phonetics and Qur'anic readings, but also a plethora of commentaries and other works by philologists, traditionalists and jurists. On the other hand, far from undergoing a certain 'pressure on the part of the orthodox' in this vast domain,[25] these variants have always assumed a sacred character, not as Qur'anic text, but as *ḥadīth āḥād*. As such they are still used by Sunnite schools.

In spite of this evidence, the picture of Christian ecclesiastical history, with which the English missionary is evidently more familiar, seems to have so much obsessed Jeffrey that he appears to transpose it almost in its entirety to the Islamic realm. In effect, the writer tries to establish in the text of the Qur'an an evolution more similar to that of the texts of the Gospels.

He begins, strangely, by distinguishing in the Qur'an, 'certain liturgical pieces' which would 'probably' have been written at the time of revelation, and other pieces which were not;[26] and by affirming, albeit contradicting himself elsewhere, that, even at the death of the Prophet, the body of revelations had not yet been collected together.[27] He goes on to deny, in a play on words, the 'official' character of Abū Bakr's recension,[28] and finally adjudges the probability of large divergences between the codices of the various metropolitan centres at the time of the ʿUthmānī decree.[29]

Jeffrey describes the Muslims of Kufa at that time as being divided into two factions: 'Some accepted the new text sent by ʿUthmān, but the larger number supported that of Ibn Masʿūd.'[30] Thus, ʿUthmān's text is presented to us not only as one among several 'rival' texts,[31] but as a parvenu, opposed not only to the older codices, but even to the reading as given at the time of the Prophet, which was finally imposed, not through its internal merits, but thanks to the prestige of Medina![32]

The grave errors revealed by this type of exposition of the history of the Qur'anic text require our thorough rectification. Let us first recall not only the maturity of the text published by ʿUthmān, but also its total identification with the recension brought together under Abū Bakr,[33] as is indeed confirmed by modern Christian research. Thus Schwally, 'We have already shown that the two editions of Zayd are identical, and the edition of ʿUthmān is nothing more than a copy of the codex of Ḥafṣa.'[34] Let us also not forget that none of the material making up the latter dates solely from the time of the first caliph; on the contrary, it can all be textually traced back to the time of the Prophet.

Coming as they do from the same source, all the variants call for equal recognition, whether in oral or written form. Thus, while it is possible that certain divergences in readings were anterior in date to those which figure in ʿUthmān's recension, for they must have become attached during some period of Muhammad's life, this relative anteriority cannot be taken to constitute a criterion of priority. The most authentic text is not necessarily the earliest, but, rather, that which was last in use; in the language of the Companions, the expression applied to extra-textual readings does not mean 'a reading from the time of the Prophet' in general, but 'the earliest reading' of the time, which is to say, the abrogated one. Thus the foundations on which people have tried to build the importance of this type of variant crumble.

Let us now leave aside these chronological gradations, for we still need to discern the most essential conditions for establishing the authenticity of a text: the assurance that its written form is sufficiently verified and vouched for by the author or his representative. It is precisely this ensemble of conditions which, at the moment of collection, rendered some variants deficient and determined their exclusion from the standard codices, and this irremediably fragile foundation was further to be shaken by the process of later transmission.

Jeffrey declares himself struck on three fronts by the uncertainties which afflict non-ʿUthmānī readings: their age – a later invention is sometimes suspected as having been falsely given early authenticity in order to benefit from the prestige of such a label;[35] the precise nature of their source – in several cases, attribution to particular authorities seems confused;[36] and the identification of their form – not only is it difficult to decide which of the diverse renderings attributed to the same reader is authentic, but in certain cases the readings seem to be linguistically impossible.[37]

Although our orientalist recognizes that non-ʿUthmānī readings are rarely attributed to authorities as figuring in their recensions, but most often as belonging simply to their oral teaching or recitation,[38] when he comes to assembling them, he takes the liberty of putting them all under the rubric of the codex. Thus he includes not only those readings which are in fact no different to the official text (as if by increasing the volume of his collection he will somehow raise its worth), but also accounts which, on the word of such and such author, are imputed only to one of their disciples.

Of what do these spurious accounts consist, and what is their importance? Let us note, first of all, that they have bearing neither on all the *sūra*s, nor on the entire extent of any one *sūra*. Under investigation, it becomes clear that spurious accounts fall into several categories:

1) interpolations made which aim to explain the implications of a word, such as *wa-Ismaʿīlu yaqūlāni* (2:127); *wa-nādāhu al-malā'ikatu yā Zakariyyā* (3:38); *ilā qawmihi fa-qāla yā qawm* (11:25); or to repeat a word already made explicit earlier, e.g. *ʿan qitāl*; *wa-ʿalā'l-ṣalā*; *wa-āmana* (2:217; 238; 285); or to develop the same sense by a paraphrase, such as *faḍlan min rabbikum fī mawāsim al-hajji fa-ibtaghū hīna'idhin* (2:198); *wa'l-ʿaṣr, wa-nawā'ib al-dahr*; *la-fī khusr, wa-innahu la-fīhi ilā ākhir al-ʿumr* (103:1-2). One can clearly see in all this the work of a commentator, moving away from the purity of the Qur'anic style and overcharging the text with excessive prolixity;

2) the substitution of a word, either for a synonym, like *yukmilu* = *yutimmu*; *yu'addūhu* = *yuwaffūhu*; *dharra* = *namla*; *al-ʿihn* = *al-ṣūf*, or for a word with a different meaning, in order to bring out the implied meaning, for example *al-ḥajja wa'l-ʿumrata li'l-bayt* instead of *al-ḥajja wa'l-ʿumrata li'llāh* (2:196);

3) simple inversion, such as *fī ẓulalin min al-ghamāmi wa'l-malā'ika* = *wa'l-malā'ikatu fī ẓulalin min al-ghamām* (2:210); *ʿalā kulli qalb* = *ʿalā qalbi kull* (40:35); *baṣīrun bi-mā taʿmalūn* = *bi-mā taʿmalūna baṣīr* (3:156);

4) on rare occasions, the omission of words, such as *bi-mithli mā āmantum* = *bi-mā āmantum* (2:137); *illā'l-sāʿata an ta'tiyahum* = *illā'l-sāʿata ta'tiyahum* (47:18).

Setting aside the matter of prejudging the respective literary value of their various lessons, one can say a priori that in the last three categories it is certainly possible that we are in the presence of equally admissible, genuine variants, the sole condition being that their origin can be historically established. In certain cases, however, one is tempted to suspect that the variant is an arrangement that has arisen in official circumstances.

The received formulation always has the merit of going beyond all particular considerations, whether of theological order (for example *bi-mithli mā āmantum*; *ya'tiyahum Allāh fī ẓulal*), political order (for example, *min al-muhājirīna wa'l-anṣāri wa-alladhīn* (9:100), and not, as ʿUmar believed it to be, *wa'l-anṣāri alladhīn*), dialectical order (for example, *inna hādhāni la-sāḥirān*), or otherwise. The only concern we see dominating the establishment of the Qur'anic text by the Companions of the Prophet is one of strict literal fidelity to each fragment as it was originally set down at the dictation of their Master, and then reread before him, to ascertain his definitive approval. It is this absolute objectivity which remains eternally in the Companions' honour.

People sometimes quibble at the case of Ibn Masʿūd or other collectors, believing that this will enable them to broach the issue of the unanimity of the Companions regarding the ʿUthmānī text. The truth is that none of the Companions contested the precision of the published text. Although there were other readings which individuals were certain had been authorized by the Prophet, without being able to bring any objective proof for this, they felt it important not to make themselves rivals. They did not wish to put these readings in the place of the formulation unanimously recognized, but chose rather to conserve them alongside the ʿUthmānī text.

Thus we see Abū Mūsā, for example, recommending to his people that they should not suppress anything to be found in his collection, and to complete anything lacking therein with the aid of the ʿUthmānī codex.[39] Similarly, when Ibn Masʿūd met with some of his dissatisfied followers, did he not remind them of the validity of all the revealed variants?[40] Their dissatisfaction, if indeed there ever was dissatisfaction,[41] no doubt had a double motive: to see this Companion deprived of the honour of being part of the committee of censors, and to be thereby obliged to deliver his manuscript for destruction. But this instinctive reaction could not be sustained for very long.

Having already been absent on official business in Iraq for a long period prior to the gathering of the recension, Ibn Masʿūd could not reasonably demand that such an urgent matter be suspended until his return *sine die*, not while other Companions also possessed documents rigorously collated and sanctioned by the Prophet. As to his own manuscript, and whether he might have inserted some private readings or some variants that had not been unanimously attested to, it had to undergo the same process as the others of its kind.[42] It ceased to be a definitive authority and became an object of limited credit and personal responsibility.

If, at a time when there had not as yet been any incidence of attempted alteration, the destruction of private manuscripts seems a little severe, it nonetheless shows the breadth of the caliph's vision. It is to his far-sightedness that Muslims owe the unity and stability of their holy Book today.[43] Even if different systems of exterior signs were introduced later (by Abū'l-Aswad al-Duwalī and his successors, Naṣr bin ʿĀṣṣim, Yaḥyā bin Yaʿmar, Ḥassan al-Baṣrī and Khalīl bin Aḥmad), the main body remains untouched, defying the effects of time.

To this day, the existence in all copies, whether written or printed, of superfluous letters, attached words and archaic spellings exclusive to Qur'anic writings, is eloquent testimony to the pious fidelity with which this monument was transmitted from generation to generation.

3
How the Qur'anic Doctrine was Announced to the World

The whole world knows what the Qur'anic doctrine we call Islam is, in a general way, but too often this is understood in very superficial terms. Islam is the name given to the religious, social and moral reform which, no sooner was it born on the coast of the Red Sea at the beginning of the seventh century of the Christian era, strode a march of victory towards north and south, east and west, until, lo and behold, after a relatively short period, it had established itself in half the then known world.

This event is one without historical precedent, and has never ceased to both fascinate humanity and excite the curiosity of historians of customs and religions. It is pointless to try to find a prototype for it in antiquity by comparing it, as some do, with the conquests of Alexander; also a rapid expansion, it is true, but one which brought with it no change to the ideas or way of life of the peoples in its wake. At the first breath of Islam, all traces of these customs would be obliterated.

We would not go so far as to suggest Alexander's influence to have been absolutely pointless – he did blaze a trail to the East, studded with beautiful cities, in which economic life became more prosperous – but it is no less true that his efforts made no mark beyond urban limits. The mass of the people, the peasants, of whom they say 'one has not truly conquered until they are conquered', retained their own character; languages, customs, political regimes and economic systems remained untouched. Even in the towns, Hellenism as embodied in the administrative framework only penetrated to any depth a small minority of the bourgeoisie.

Does one have to add that the Greek colonies were not long in falling into the hands of other conquerors and that, under the Roman Empire, these towns fell into progressive stages of ruin? Just one or two well-known dates suffice to bring home the ephemeral nature of Alexander's disparate edifice.

By some twenty years after the death of Alexander, around 301 BC, his empire had been divided into three kingdoms. From here on, a progressive mutilation took place: after fifty years Upper Asia was taken over by the Parthians (250 BC); sixty years later, Asia Minor fell under Roman domination (190 BC); another fifty years, and Palestine had become an independent Jewish state (144-64 BC); towards the same date the metropolitan centre itself (Greece in 146 BC and Macedonia in 142 BC) was reduced to a Roman province; if the royalty of Egypt remained to one side for longer and did not suffer the yoke of Rome until 31 BC, her political decline had already begun after the first three Ptolemies (221 BC).

But the heart of the matter does not lie here. Let us leave aside the material aspect of Alexander's civilization and look at events from an ideological standpoint: it is undeniable that the Macedonian conqueror, far from bringing with him a Greek ideology, purely and simply adopted the current ideas of the conquered countries and affiliated himself with their divinities.

During the two main periods of the Greek and Roman empires, generally speaking, the philosophical and religious ideas which were flourishing at this time in the East, and especially in Alexandria, did not contain any Hellenic importation. On the contrary, they were essentially oriental doctrines making use of a Greek vehicle to be conveyed into Europe under the name of neo-platonism or Christianity. One could almost say that the Orient conquered its conquerors in this respect.

When Islam arrived on the scene, not just the political and economic façade, but the very foundation of the human soul was changed in entire peoples, almost overnight. Languages, thoughts, laws, aspirations, customs, people's view of the world and of God, everything was transformed at a stroke.[1] This conquest of the spirit not only entranced the souls which it penetrated; it continued to gain new territory in every place where its simplicity and primitive purity were displayed.

This statement hardly squares up with the widespread opinion, a thousand times repeated, that Islam spread through the force of arms alone. Indeed, the ascendancy which Islam maintains even at the present time is surely tangible proof that it acts upon the spirit by virtue of an internal force, and that it has a particular affinity with human nature and truth.

At one time, it is true, when antagonistic powers were pouring all their hatred and violence into persecuting and torturing Islam's nascent doctrine, Islam found herself obliged to react in order to put an end to an injustice which had lasted long enough. Once resistance was declared, and reactionary elements rose up from every part in an attempt to form a coalition against the new order, poised to supplant them, blows succeeded blows, and time needed to pass before peace could be re-established. Yet an investigation of this episode cannot lead us to the essential, or intentional, factor that accounts for the spread of the Islamic message.

The first ten years of Muhammad's teaching do not only show us how the simple exposition of the doctrine, in spite of all the obstacles, was able to bring about new conversions every day. They also display with what valour and to what extremes the Master and his disciples were prepared to endure the mockery and insults of their compatriots, the isolation from all public contact, sometimes even cruel torture and suffering:

> ... *not he who is compelled while his heart is content with faith* ...
>
> 16:106

> ... *but when he is persecuted for the sake of Allāh* ...
>
> 29:10

About a hundred of the first Muslims, including some of the most noble, like ʿUthmān and the daughter of Abū Sufyān, Umm Ḥabība, were eventually obliged to seek refuge with the king of Abyssinia:

> ... *those who flee after they are persecuted* ...
>
> 16:110

The inhabitants of Yathrib (later called Medina) provide for us the most striking illustration of the prodigious effect this peaceful call was capable of producing: long before seeing Muhammad's face or hearing his voice, on the basis of having simply heard the Qur'anic message via their pilgrims, the Medinese Arabs welcomed Islam with such enthusiasm that there was no family which did not count amongst its number several believers. What is more, all the divisions and hostilities which had reigned in their midst for a quarter of a century were suddenly extinguished as if by a Divine breath:[2]

> *And He has united their hearts. If thou hadst spent all that is in the earth, thou couldst not have united their hearts, but Allāh united them* ...
>
> 8:63

Those who had been relentless enemies became brothers:

> ... *And remember Allāh's favour to you when you were enemies, then He united your hearts so by His favour you became brethren.*
>
> 3:102

Islamic institutions which could not be openly performed in Mecca were immediately, communally, and in broad daylight practised in Yathrib (hence the Friday prayer led by Abū Amāma a whole year before the Hijra). Accordingly, nearly all of the faithful, all of whom had to a greater or lesser extent been persecuted in Mecca, abandoned *their homes and their possessions*,[3] and came to be received into this welcoming and hospitable environment. Everything had taken place peaceably and with dignity, at least on the part of the Muslims, and there was nothing to suggest a breakout of violence.

Thus reassured about the fate of his disciples, Muhammad did not hasten to join them. Regardless of the possible danger which menaced his person, the Prophet did not wish to leave his position of duty without an express authorization from revelation. Until that day he felt he should stay in Mecca and continue to preach in his native country. So he remained alone with his two friends, Abū Bakr and ʿAlī.

It was on the evening of the great plot hatched against his life that Muhammad received the Divine order to leave; at the very hour the perfidious project went into execution, the Prophet discreetly left town. One of his two friends accompanied him, the other was entrusted with covering their traces. But, having miraculously escaped from danger, should Muhammad not have thought of wreaking vengeance upon the enemies who had tried to kill him? Certainly not.

If we look at the stages of Muhammad's activity during the first year of the Hijra and a good part of the second, we find his efforts devoted, not to revenge, but to sacred and constructive works: the prescription of the fast, the institution of the call to prayer, the construction of the mosque, and the inner and peaceful organization of society. Everything seemed to indicate that from that time onwards the Muslims were going to turn their backs on their former territory – even in the direction of their prayer.

Then, towards the middle of the second year, the Muslims began to intercept convoys of merchandise belonging to their former persecutors in order to confront them. Whence this reversal, this sudden change of attitude?

We cannot, and the impartial judgements of the orientalists agree on this point, attribute this change to the personal psychology of the Prophet. Belligerent measures were simply not a part of his character, quite the reverse; the indulgence and solicitude he showed towards his adversaries brought Qur'anic reproaches down upon him:

> *Ask forgiveness for them or ask not forgiveness for them. Even if thou ask forgiveness for them seventy times, Allāh will not forgive them …*
>
> 9:80

> *It is not for the Prophet and those who believe to ask forgiveness for the polytheists, even though they should be near relatives, after it has become clear to them that they are companions of the flaming fire.*
>
> 9:113

In the Tradition there are preserved many accounts of Muhammad's acts of clemency in the face of crimes committed both against him and against those around him.[4]

Some have tried then to explain this new orientation as the result of pressure exerted upon the Prophet by his people, whose warrior spirit would surely be their most essential characteristic. Yet scholars who have penetrated more deeply into the Arab psyche find themselves unable to support this hypothesis; on the contrary, they have shown to what extent the spilling of blood provoked horror, even among desert Arabs. The Bedouin do not seek war, they tell us, but if it is imposed upon them they will accept it rather than shame and humiliation. Even during the frequent raids they perpetrated upon one other, nomadic tribes took the utmost care to avoid any bloody incident.[55] Thus, neither in the psychology of the people nor in that of their leader do we find a satisfactory explanation for the new turn of events.

We shall look next at historical fact. Surely something must have occurred to bring about such a reaction? As a matter of fact, the Qur'an does make us party to an extremely provoking scene. When the exodus took place, the Prophet himself delayed his departure from Mecca until the very last possible moment. One can be sure that he left behind no outstanding matters needing attention, no possible hope of a last-minute convert in that self-opiniated city. In truth, there were none.

Yet this is how the Qur'an makes us hear the anguished cry of the Muslims left in Mecca, without support, suffering for their faith and calling on the help of God against their oppressors:

> *Our Lord, take us out of this town, whose people are oppressors, and grant us from Thee a friend, and grant us from Thee a helper!*
>
> 4:75

Despite the absence of any further communication, the old seeds of teaching and example eventually bore fruit. Faith came into being and, as it pulsated with life, fierceness and cruelty were unleashed in an attempt to suffocate it, choosing as always the most defenseless of victims.

Did the emigrants and their hosts, enjoying as they did full liberty of faith and ritual, have the right to shut their eyes and remain indifferent to the fate of their brothers? Could one reasonably, and without prejudice, deny truth and virtue their right to be saved, even if one would thereby enable despotism to take up arms?

Material help, however rightfully demanded, was not lightly undertaken by the Muslims, at least not in its truly warlike form. It suffices for us to consult our source of documentation par excellence, whose authenticity and historical fidelity cannot be called into question by any scholar – the Qur'an. There one can quite plainly see how the the 'liberated' hesitated in the face of a military project to liberate the 'captives'. We see their hatred of war:

> *Fighting is enjoined on you, though it is disliked by you …*
>
> 2:216

their instinct for the conservation of life:

> *… Our Lord, why hast Thou ordained fighting for us? Wouldst Thou not grant us respite to a near term? Say: The enjoyment of this world is short, and the Hereafter is better for him who keeps his duty. And you shall not be wronged a whit.*
>
> 4:77

but also the particularly difficult circumstances which made warfare seem almost absurd in their eyes.

'To launch ourselves unexpectedly against an enemy that is already marching on us and is vastly superior to us in numbers and equipment?

> *Indeed there was a sign for you in the two hosts (which) met together in encounter – one party fighting in the way of Allāh and the other disbelieving, whom they saw twice as many as themselves with the sight of the eye …*
>
> 3:12

'Would it not be better to content ourselves with some indirect measure of reprisal,[6] something to alert the Qurayshites to our reaction and make them decide to spare our brothers? It would be better to intercept our adversary's merchant caravan than suffer the shock of his army!'

> *… and you loved that the one not armed should be yours …*
>
> 8:7

Such was the line of reasoning taken in the Muslim camp.

But the imperative of duty was there. The hour of supreme commitment had sounded. The time had come for God to settle the debate between truth and falsehood:

> *That He might cause the Truth to triumph and bring the falsehood to naught*
> 8:8

Man could do nothing but resign himself, in order that each one would know why he should live or why he should die:

> *In order that Allāh might bring about a matter which had to be done; that he who perished by clear argument might perish ...*
> 8:42

for his ideals, or for his idols:

> *Those who believe fight in the way of Allāh, and those who disbelieve fight in the way of the devil ...*
> 4:76

Such were the circumstances into which flashed the first spark of the idea of armed struggle.

During their time in Mecca, while instances of persecution remained individual and sporadic, the Muslims were anxious to endure their wounds courageously and avoid any violent reaction. But now that the pagan aggression was becoming a systematic campaign, the faithful were first authorized:

> *Permission (to fight) is given to those on whom war is made, because they are oppressed ...*
> 22:39

and then urged:[7]

> *Fighting is enjoined on you ...*
> 2:216

to defend themselves as a community, and, above all, to relieve those among them who were without protection:

> *... the weak among the men and the women and the children ...*
> 4:75

In all objectivity, we cannot reproach such a devout attitude, concerned solely with self-defence.

Our next question, then, is whether Qur'anic legislation evolved as a consequence of this situation. Did it extend the right of self-defence into the arena of attack?

The western world seems badly informed on this point. It is generally believed that the sacred Book gives Muslims the right, even the duty, to employ arms, both in order to impose their doctrine and in order to eliminate those who do not adopt it. To this concept the name holy war has been given, a term which has been made to correspond with the Qur'anic word *jihād*.

Yet the truth is that this generic term for 'effort' has nothing specifically military about it; we find it used in the Meccan *sūra*s to designate a constructive effort made to preach and persuade peacefully:

> *So obey not the disbelievers, and strive against them a mighty striving with it.*
>
> 25:52

also to signify a purely personal moral effort:

> *And those who strive hard for Us, We shall certainly guide them in Our ways. And Allāh is surely with the doers of good.*
>
> 29:69

The term which properly signifies 'fight' is *qitāl*.

Furthermore, a quick glance at the text shows us quite plainly the objective, the aim and the limits assigned by Qur'anic law to such a fight:

> *And fight in the way of Allāh against those who fight against you but be not aggressive. Surely Allāh loves not the aggressors.*
>
> 2:190

> *But if they desist, then surely Allāh is Forgiving, Merciful ... if they desist, then there should be no hostility except against the oppressors.*
>
> 2:192-3

> *... if they withdraw from you and fight you not and offer you peace, then Allāh allows you no way against them. You will find others who desire to be secure from you and secure from their own people. Whenever they are made to return to hostility, they are plunged into it. So if they withdraw not from you, nor offer you peace and restrain their hands, then seize them and kill them wherever you find them. And against these We have given you a clear authority.*
>
> 4:90-1

We find the same distinction elsewhere:

> *Allāh forbids you not respecting those who fight you not for religion, nor drive you forth from your homes, that you show them kindness and deal with them justly. Surely Allāh loves the doers of justice. Allāh forbids you only respecting those who fight you for religion, and drive you forth from your homes and help (others) in your expulsion, that you make friends of them; and whoever makes friends of them, these are the wrongdoers.*
>
> 60:8-9

Indeed, even in *Sūrat al-Barā'at*, where the Qur'an is at its most severe against the unfaithful, the hypocrites and the spineless, commencing as it does with a solemn proclamation of the break with the polytheists, we can see what care the text takes to exclude those who have not violated their treaty from punitive measures:

> *Except those of the idolaters with whom you have made an agreement, then they have not failed you in anything and have not backed up anyone against you; so fulfil their agreement to the end of their term. Surely Allāh loves those who keep their duty.*
>
> 9:4

The object of the fight to which the Qur'an urges its adherents is even more closely defined in verse 13 of the same *sūra*:

> *Will you not fight a people who broke their oaths and aimed at the expulsion of the Messenger, and they attacked you first? Do you fear them? But Allāh has more right that you should fear Him, if you are believers.*
>
> 9:13

It goes without saying that Muslims should:

> *...fight the polytheists all together as they fight you all together. And know that Allāh is with those who keep their duty.*
>
> 9:36

But:

> *... So as long as they are true to you, be true to them. Surely Allāh loves those who keep their duty.*
>
> 9:7

At no point in the Qur'an do we find the legitimization of initiated violence. It describes only the reinstation of justice as adapted to the attitude of the partners. What is more, the Qur'an enjoins the Prophet to faithfully reassure even those who are not joined with the Muslims by any pact, yet ask for protection:[8]

And if anyone of the idolaters seek thy protection, protect him till he hears the word of Allāh, then convey him to his place of safety ...

9:6

All the responsibility for a war, then, falls on the person who strikes the first blow. But how far does this responsibility extend? Is it a question of a collective responsibility? We have shown elsewhere that the Qur'anic principle of responsibility, moral as well as penal, is purely individual;[9] and that civil responsibility has a very strong tendency towards the same idea. We could say as much about military responsibility.

When the Qur'an says 'fight against those who fight you', it is only referring to those who can effectively enter into armed combat. Tradition goes to great lengths to plainly establish this issue: women, children, old people, the blind, the infirm, foreigners, peasants in their fields and hermits in their cells are all granted immunity against hostilities.[10]

Another restriction is the forbidding of all operations which would lead to overall destruction, such as flooding or fire, and the Qur'anic commandment that those who have ceased to fight should be pardoned, upheld by the Prophet to the extent that he even forbade the pursuit of an enemy in flight. What, then is the aim of this legislation? Simply to avoid one danger.

Islam wholeheartedly condemns the spirit of destruction and domination:

That abode of the Hereafter, We assign it to those who have no desire to exalt themselves in the earth nor to make mischief. And the good end is for those who keep their duty.

28:83

It does not even wish to impose a universal ideology:

And if thy Lord had pleased, all those who are in the earth would have believed, all of them. Wilt thou then force men till they are believers?

10:99

and, even if it did, this would be impossible to achieve.

Indeed, the founder of Islam should have had no illusions about human possibilities, for the Qur'an fixed the limits on his perspectives. Can he change the will of God if it is by a Divine decree that:

And if thy Lord had pleased, He would have made people a single nation.

And they cease not to differ, except those on whom thy Lord has mercy ...
11:118-9

and that:

And most men believe not, though thou desirest it eagerly.
12:103

Islam has no wish to force consciences or to shackle freedom in matters of faith:

There is no compulsion in religion ...
2:256

On the contrary, it is opposed to those who try to stifle freedom and put it to harsh tests:

... Persecution is graver than slaughter. And they will not cease fighting you until they turn you back from your religion, if they can ...
2:217

To break this fetter was the liberal, dispassionate intention that inspired the warriors:

And fight them until there is no persecution, and religion is only for Allāh
2:193

And fight with them until there is no more persecution, and all religions are for Allāh ...
8:39

Does this mean then that the salvation or damnation of others should leave Muslims cold? This is the explanation some have tried to give for this spirit of clemency towards people of other denominations.[11] But this, too, is nothing but another way of misrepresenting the true character of Qur'anic doctrine. One either has too much or too little proselytism; is either a fanatic or indifferent.

In reality, the Qur'an does not fall into either of these extremes. It is a duty to preach the truth and to exhort people to follow virtue:

And from among you there should be a party who invite to good and enjoin the right and forbid the wrong. And these are they who are successful.
3:104

> *... and exhort one another to Truth, and exhort one another to patience.*
> 103:3

and to do this energetically:

> *... strive against them a mighty striving with it.*
> 25:52

But these exhortations must be made in the wisest, most persuasive, gentlest manner possible:

> *Call to the way of thy Lord with wisdom and goodly exhortation, and argue with them in the best manner ...*
> 16:125

One's duty in this area does not consist of constraint, but of the demonstration of what one believes to be true. The other is then free to believe or not believe, provided only that he or she allows those who do believe the liberty to venerate their own ideal and give it the radiance it deserves. The rest is each person's individual responsibility:

> *Their guidance is not thy duty, but Allāh guides whom He pleases ...*
> 2:272

> *... he who errs cannot harm you when you are on the right way ...*
> 5:105

The legal principle which determines the relationship between the Muslim community and other nations and faiths is generally summed up by the word 'tolerance'. In certain respects, however, this term could be considered as less than the truth.

First of all, people who do not adopt Islam but do submit themselves peaceably to its civil law are not only tolerated, they are guaranteed respect for their territory and its members (their persons, goods, religions and customs). Furthermore, Islam takes it upon itself to assure such liberties to these non-believers on the same level as it does to its own subjects.

Secondly, for those who neither accept the faith nor the law of the Muslims, the Qur'an specifies no more than an inoffensive attitude. In return it provides them the most generous treatment, founded at the same time on justice and benevolence:

> *... show them kindness and deal with them justly. Surely Allāh loves the doers of justice.*
> 60:8

Positive resistance is only imposed in default of these three solutions of religious community, social unity and good neighbourliness. When unbelief strikes out against belief and tries to persecute and annihilate it en masse, is it conceivable that religion should stand passively by, arms folded, watching her own demise?

Whoever would claim another goal for this kind of fighting is asked to give us an approximate number of the proselytes gained for Islam by such severe methods. Very early on, the first Muslims had both types of experience and stated that there was nothing more valuable to the faith than the peaceful, free exchange of ideas. They understood this too well to then try to impose their religion on others by force. During the truce of al-Ḥudaybiyya, we are told, more people were converted thanks to the opening of the frontiers than in all the preceding years taken together.

One could certainly suppose that some mistakes were made, and that, moreover, they would be inevitable in periods of confusion; one could even suspect there might have been some deviation of intent over subsequent generations. But first let us listen to the assertions of a contemporary critic who was not even in favour of Muslim rule.[12]

'In spite of official obstacles put in the way of conversion,' he says,[13] 'mass conversion took place';[14] 'Never had the Arab, in all the ardour of his new-found faith, thought of extinguishing a concurrent faith in blood';[15] 'Towards the Christians, as towards the Manicheans, the caliph never allowed persecution.'[16]

Quite hypothetically, with the miseries to be deplored during the Islamic conquests so relatively small and the operations so rapid, one sometimes gets the impression that doors were already half-open, and the conquerors had only to push them open. This speed, and the subsequent immediate establishment of order and a reign of justice, saved many a mortal and material loss. The Protestant Reformation, which was concerned only with a few articles of Christianity, cost Europe more: a century and a half of deplorable evils and grief.

An artificial construction, that might live for a moment by virtue of acquired strength, will disintegrate as soon as the foreign elements which contributed towards its building disappear. Now, what do we see today, more than 12 centuries after the cessation of Islamic expansion?

The Islamic institution – spread among peoples of different race, language, colour, climate, from China to Morocco, and from Lithuania to Mozambique, representing more than a sixth of the world population,[17] exposed over the centuries to all the interior and exterior agencies of destruction – has not lost very much on the surface, and certainly has lost nothing at all of its depth. In spite of its political vicissitudes, Islam's religious and moral edifice remains intact.

Islam is so solid that one could go so far as to say, 'there has not been a single example since the beginning of the Exodus of a Muhammadan converted to another religion',[18] or, at least, affirm with certitude that Muslims are much less disposed to put aside their beliefs than practitioners of any other religion. Would it not be underestimating the laws of the psyche to simply attribute this undefecting attachment to a kind of atavistic process? A simple constraint once exerted over their most distant ancestors, the memory of which they now carry engraved on their very cerebral structure?

We are forced to admit the existence of certain intrinsic qualities which have allowed Islam such extension and such permanence, so far from its cradle.

Part Two
The Qur'an from its Three Main Aspects: Religion, Morality and Literature

If therefore, far from any outside influence, the Qur'an still has an amazing effect on many minds, this must be because it presents a particular attraction for man. It must adapt itself to their true manner of thinking and feeling, answer their requirements of belief and action, and bring an exact solution to the great problems which disturb them. In a word, it must be able to give complete satisfaction to their need for truth, goodness and beauty, through a Work that is at the same time religious, moral and literary.

4
Truth, or the Religious Element

One of the major reasons that Islamic preaching has such power to inspire is, in our opinion, because of the way it presents the truths of religion and attempts to bring to a conclusion disputes on this subject.

The revealed religions, so-called, having once given a precise answer to the two great theoretical questions which have divided and subdivided philosophic thought – 'What is the origin of the world?' and 'Where is it going?' – have built systems of cult and dogma on top of their responses. These systems have varied from one epoch to another, and from one community to another, and still change beneath our very eyes, not only in their forms, but also in their fundamental principles.

By a kind of instinctive logic, man does not easily admit that one Divine truth could contradict another. Can something that was yesterday declared to be the truth for all eternity, tomorrow be declared outdated? Can it be rejected and replaced by its opposite without disturbing our spirit and leading us to suspect falseness in one affirmation or the other?

However superficial this might seem, whatever the experts settle on for this or that idea will remain for the masses a sign of its truth. From this angle, one could say that a doctrine has more of an edge over souls the more authorities it rallies to uphold its system and thus augment people's confidence in it. The disputes of teachers disconcert us and send us into disarray; it is in their unanimity that we are able to find the balance and interior repose necessary to us. How comforting it is to know that others think exactly as we do, that the great minds of humanity meet, that those who transmit the Word of God confirm each other and show solidarity. Does not Moses ceaselessly refer back to Abraham, Isaac and Jacob? Did not Jesus come to confirm the previous prophets and laws?

With even more forcefulness and tenacity does the Qur'an insist upon this issue. It categorically states, not only that all prophets constitute one indivisible religious community under the aegis of the Lord:

> *Surely this your community is a single community, and I am your Lord, so serve Me.*
>
> 21:92

> *And surely this your community is one community, and I am your Lord, so keep your duty to Me.*
>
> 23:52

but that this unity in ancient times belonged to all men.

It was their successors who became divided from one another:

> *... And if Allāh had pleased, those after them would not have fought one with another after clear arguments had come to them ...*
>
> 2:253

> *And (all) people are but a single nation, then they disagree.*
>
> 10:19

either by forgetting one aspect of the Divine teaching:

> ... [they] *neglect a portion of that whereof they were reminded ...*
>
> 5:13

> *... they neglected a portion of that whereof they were reminded ...*
>
> 5:14

or by presenting it wrongly:

> *... a party from among them indeed used to hear the word of Allāh, then altered it after they had understood it, and they know (this).*
>
> 2:75

> *... they alter the words from their places ...*
>
> 5:13

through their own ambition and self-interest:

> *... And a party of them surely conceal the truth while they know.*
>
> 2:146

Those who conceal aught of the Book that Allāh has revealed and take for it a small price …

2:174

Following its own inner logic, the Qur'an does not define Islam as a Muhammadan rival against the Mosaic or the Christian, disputing the trustworthiness and truthfulness of the latter: to be Muslim means to belong at the same time to Moses, to Jesus and to all the Divine messengers since the creation of humankind. Islam puts past prophets side by side, accords them the same respect and gives equal credence to their teachings. It makes no distinction between them:

Or were you witnesses when death visited Jacob, when he said to his sons: What will you serve after me? They said: We shall serve thy God and the God of thy fathers, Abraham and Ishmael and Isaac, one God only, and to Him do we submit.

2:133

The Messenger believes in what has been revealed to him from his Lord, and (so do) the believers. They all believe in Allāh and His angels and His Books and His messengers. We make no difference between any of His messengers …

2:285

Say: We believe in Allāh and that which is revealed to us, and that which was revealed to Abraham and Ishmael and Isaac and Jacob and the tribes, and that which was given to Moses and Jesus and to the prophets from their Lord; we make no distinction between any of them, and to Him we submit.

3:83

And those who believe in Allāh and His messengers and make no distinction between any of them, to them He will grant their rewards. And Allāh is ever Forgiving, Merciful.

4:152

Or rather, it emphasizes that we belong to God and should follow His Will as it is manifested through their lips.[1]

Accordingly, the Qur'an calls for the cessation of schism and rivalry:

As for those who split up their religion and became sects, thou hast no concern with them. Their affair is only with Allāh, then He will inform them of what they did.

6:160

He has made plain to you the religion which He enjoined upon Noah and which We have revealed to thee, and which We enjoined on Abraham and Moses and Jesus – to establish religion and not to be divided therein …

42:13

After all, if the doctrine which a certain man has just preached were identical to mine, there would be no reason for me to reject his words except egoism:

And when it is said to them, Believe in that which Allāh has revealed, they say: We believe in that which was revealed to us. And they deny what is besides that, while it is the Truth verifying that which they have …

2:91

jealousy:

Many of the people of the Book wish that they could turn you back into disbelievers after you have believed, out of envy …

2:109

or vanity:

And the Jews and the Christians say: We are the sons of Allāh and His beloved ones …

5:18

The Qur'an thus appeals for a return to the primordial unity – a union which all good souls long for and cherish, the pronunciation of whose name opens those hearts that are well-disposed to it – a first step, maybe, but one on whose programme and method everything resides.

We believe that the starting point, the kernel around which the Qur'an's system of argument is organized, consists of the central idea of a transcendent, all-powerful, all-beneficent Artisan, Who has created all things in the world and on Whom everything depends.

The beauty of this central idea lies both in the fact that it fits perfectly with the proposed concept of religious unity, schism only being able to arise in a pluralistic situation:

Say: O People of the Book, come to an equitable word between us and you, that we shall serve none but Allāh and that we shall not associate aught with Him, and that some of us shall not take others for lords besides Allāh. But if they turn away, then say: Bear witness, We are Muslims.

3:63

And argue not with the People of the Book except by what is best, save such of them as act unjustly. But say: We believe in that which has been revealed to us and revealed to you, and our God and your God is One, and to Him we submit.

24:46

and in its rising above all considerations of religious particularities.

The Qur'an quite simply calls all men to the eternal truth, that which has never ceased to be recognized, and is indeed easily recognizable to all: even the pagan Arabs, who had lowered themselves to gross idolatry, did not any the less recognize a supreme Deity, Creator of the universe and Administrator of the celestial world:

And if thou ask them, Who created the heavens and the earth and made the sun and the moon subservient? They would say, Allāh …

29:61

This recognition is not due to some residual vestige of the patriarchal faith of Abraham and Ismāʿīl; it exists as a seed in the human spirit. All souls swear to it before taking up their bodies:

And when thy Lord brought forth from the children of Adam, from their loins, their descendants, and made them bear witness about themselves: Am I not your Lord? They said: Yes; we bear witness …

7:172

But this primordial monotheism, what the Qur'an calls *the right religion*,[2] was only a kind of theoretical view, enveloped and practically submerged by an infinity of cults to inferior divinities:

And most of them believe not in Allāh without associating others (with Him).

12:106

God was only invoked in situations of grave danger:

He it is Who makes you travel by land and sea; until, when you are in the ships, and they sail on with them in a pleasant breeze, and they rejoice at it, a violent wind overtakes them and the billows surge in on them from all sides, and they deem that they are encompassed about. Then they pray to Allāh, being sincere to Him in obedience: If Thou deliver us from this, we will certainly be of the grateful ones.

10:22

and they only consecrated a tiny part of their offerings to Him:

> *And they set apart a portion for Allāh out of what He has created of tilth and cattle …*
>
> 6:137

Through their daily contact with the elements of nature, the pagan Arabs could not prevent themselves from attributing some Divine power to the stars:

> *And that He is the Lord of Sirius*
>
> 53:49

and planets:

> *… Adore not the sun nor the moon, but adore Allāh Who created them …*
>
> 41:37

before which they prostrated themselves.

Between God and man they instituted intermediary powers, capable of bringing man closer to his Creator:

> *… And those who choose protectors besides Him (say): We serve them only that they may bring us nearer to Allāh …*
>
> 39:3

or of interceding in man's favour before God:

> *And they serve besides Allāh that which can neither harm them nor profit them, and they say: These are our intercessors with Allāh …*
>
> 10:18

Thus the angels, which they took to be the daughters of God, were an object of their adoration:

> *And they make the angels, who are the servants of the Beneficent, females … And they say: If the Beneficent had pleased, we should not have worshipped them …*
>
> 43:19-20

similarly statues:

> *… so shun the filth of the idols and shun false words.*
>
> 22:30

and raised slabs of stone:

> *O you who believe, intoxicants and games of chance and (sacrificing to) stones set up and (dividing by) arrows are only an uncleanness, the devil's work; so shun it …*
>
> 5:90

These symbols, which were meant to conceal hidden principles, or carry invisible deities in their eyes, ended up by receiving the same veneration as that Reality which they were meant to symbolize. Beneath the ultimate creator God, the superstitious imagination invented, little by little, an infinity of smaller gods for lesser affairs. How could this inveterate tendency to anthropomorphize conceive of a King, without adding to Him aides and collaborators, as worthy as the Creator of being adored?

Tradition has conserved a marvellous formulation of just such a conception, where the created deities are at the same time possession and associate of God the Creator. Pagan pilgrims used the following in their invocations: 'I consecrate myself to You, O God! I consecrate myself to You. You have no associate other than the ones over which You are absolute Master – as much as You are over everything that depends on it.'

That all the gods should in the end be One would have seemed strange to the pagan Arabs:

> *Makes he the gods a single God? Surely this is a strange thing.*
>
> 38:5

even more so because they would never before have heard this unity of God preached, either from amongst themselves or in the preceding revelation (the Christianity that was introduced into Arabia from the north and the south by certain refugee sects):

> *We never heard of this in the former faith: this is nothing but a forgery.*
>
> 38:7

In spite of regional differences between the gods worshipped, there was sufficient linkage between them for us to deduce that the Arabs did practise a crude form of polytheism:

> *And when the son of Mary is mentioned as an example, lo! Thy people raise a clamour thereat. And they say: Are our gods better, or is he? They set it forth to thee only by way of disputation. Nay, they are a contentious people.*
>
> 43:57-8

Even people who possessed their own holy Scriptures had somehow managed to reconcile the unity of God the Creator with the plurality of the worshipped gods.

The Qur'an seized upon the first concept in order to destroy the second. It takes up its adversaries on their own avowals to show them, if not their absurdity, at least their ingratitude in perpetrating such confusion of thought:

> *O men, serve your Lord Who created you and those before you, so that you may guard against evil, Who made the earth a resting-place for you and the heaven a structure, and sends down rain from the clouds then brings forth with it fruits for your sustenance; so do not set up rivals to Allāh while you know.*
>
> 2:21-2

> *And if Allāh afflicts thee with harm, there is none to remove it but He; and if He intends good to thee, there is none to repel His grace. He brings it to whom He pleases of His servants …*
>
> 10:107

> *O people, a parable is set forth, so listen to it. Surely those whom you call upon besides Allāh cannot create a fly, though they should all gather for it. And if the fly carry off aught from them, they cannot take it back from it. Weak are (both) the invoker and the invoked.*
>
> 22:73

Thus the unity which the Qur'an teaches is based on a pre-existing idea which already had a place, buried beneath many conflicting theories, in people's minds. Islam does not discover it, nor piece it together from several fragments, but rather disengages it from the midst of chaos and returns it once more to purity. The Qur'an proceeds in this case by elimination, not by addition.

As we intimated above, the power of a religious idea rests, not in its originality, but in its having come from the origin. The further its roots go back into the beliefs of our most distant ancestors, the more it inspires our enthusiasm and attachment. That is why, in addition to the deductive reasoning we have just indicated, the Qur'an rests its doctrine of unity on the prophetic tradition of all epochs:

> *… They said: We shall serve thy God and the God of thy fathers, Abraham and Ishmael and Isaac, one God only …*
>
> 2:133

> *It is not meet for a mortal that Allāh should give him the Book and the judgement and the prophethood, then he should say to men: Be my servants*

besides Allāh's; but (he would say): Be worshippers of the Lord because you teach the Book and because you study (it).

3:78

Or, have they taken gods besides Him? Say: Bring your proof. This [the Qur'an] *is the reminder of those with me and the reminder of those before me ... And We sent no messenger before thee but We revealed to him that there is no God but Me, so serve Me.*

21:24-5

... [yours is] *the faith of your father Abraham. He named you Muslims ...*

22:78

And ask those of Our messengers whom We sent before thee: Did We ever appoint gods to be worshipped besides the Beneficent?

43:45

Thus reason and tradition converge to establish the cult of the unique God and refute idolatry and association in all its forms:

Say: Have you considered that which you invoke besides Allāh? Show me what they have created of the earth, or have they a share in the heavens? Bring me a Book before this or any relics of knowledge, if you are truthful.

46:4

But how do we explain why such a rational, primordial proposition, constantly renewed by positive teachings, vanished from the spirit of man and ceded its place to totally opposing ideas? The answer is that man, by his very nature, is moved to admire creative power, wherever it manifests itself. The process then moves imperceptibly, with no clear separation of stages, from admiration to adoration.

Thus, for instance, the sun which illumines us, heats us and gives us life; the tree which shelters us and gratifies us with its fruits; the fountain which spurts mysteriously in the middle of the rocks – all these silent, efficacious natural powers are capable of captivating the spirit of the person who gives them their attention.

And what about the extraordinary, supernatural wonders of a magician? Led most often by the exterior senses, it is easy for intelligence to attribute these phenomena to their immediate milieu, to attribute them to the object which manifests them, as though it were a real, effective, autonomous creature.

It is only through a deliberate, voluntary act of reflection that intelligence is able to rise above the phenomenon before one's eyes, to view its origins; to move from sensibility to intelligence. One of the first aims of the Qur'an is to encourage this act of reflection. It ceaselessly reminds us that no creature, in heaven or on earth, is capable of emerging from nothingness without God's creative act. Self-creation, or the creation of anything outside oneself, is an impossibility:

> *Or were they created without a (creative) agency? Or are they the creators? Or did they create the heavens and the earth? Nay, they are sure of nothing.*
>
> 52:35-6

> *Do they associate (with Him) that which has created naught, while they are themselves created? And they cannot give them help, nor can they help themselves.*
>
> 7:191-2

What is more, if a fly took something from the most powerful creature in the world, he or she would be incapable of recovering it. Nothing but God possesses *the weight of an atom* in the heavens or on earth, neither as His partner nor as His helper:

> *Say: Call upon those whom you assert besides Allāh; they control not the weight of an atom in the heavens or in the earth, nor have they any partnership in either, nor has He a helper among them.*
>
> 34:22

No one but God can change the order of nature:

> *That was the way of Allāh concerning those who have gone before; and thou wilt find no change in the way of Allāh.*
>
> 33:62

> *... But thou wilt find no alteration in the course of Allāh; and thou wilt find no change in the course of Allāh.*
>
> 35:43

> *(Such has been) the course of Allāh that has run before, and thou wilt not find a change in Allāh's course.*
>
> 48:23

nor maintain it:

> *... And He withholds the heaven from falling on the earth except with His permission ...*
>
> 22:65

> *Surely Allāh upholds the heavens and the earth lest they come to naught. And if they come to naught, none can uphold them after Him ...*
>
> 35:41

We call this constant order of things, proof against any human intervention, the inexorable laws. This constancy, and all the laws of causality, depend only upon one word from the Creator. If He wishes He can make the rainwater salty and bitter, or make the sky fall upon the earth, or make mankind disappear and put other creatures in its place:

> *... If He please, He will take you away and bring a new creation.*
>
> 14:19

Who could arrest His arm if He wished to bring everything that lives on earth to ruin?

> *... Say: Who then could control anything as against Allāh when He wished to destroy the Messiah, son of Mary, and his mother and all those on the earth? ...*
>
> 5:17

God is not just the most mighty; He is the Almighty. The entire chain of direct and indirect events is nothing but an instrument in the all-powerful hand of the World Artificer:

> *Allāh is the Creator of all things and He has charge over everything. His are the treasures of the heavens and the earth ...*
>
> 39:62-3

In the final analysis, God is the explanation for everything:

> *To thy Lord on that day is the driving.*
>
> 75:30

Such language might tempt one to believe in absolute fatalism, where all human intervention is in vain, and realms are entirely passive, all connection with their causality disappeared. Yet such a conclusion, as well as disconcerting reason and stifling knowledge, is in opposition to two groups of Qur'anic texts: those which make a constant appeal to our moral efforts and those which explain one physical or historical phenomenon by another.

The only tenable solution would seem to be one which allows to each of these givens a defined scope: not to attribute to man and the world any autonomous power, nor yet to condemn them to absolute impotence. This is the golden mean at which the Qur'an seems to want to place us.

If a series of phenomena are always produced in a regular, ordered sequence, we have the right to suppose that they will produce themselves in the same order in the future. Belief in a stable order in nature is indispensable to life. But one should not believe that this stability resides in the things themselves, independent of the Higher Spirit which governs and coordinates them. Everything owes its existence, its continuance, its power and its stability to the Divine Will.

The religious explanation of the world, far from showing a laziness of spirit, proceeds from a higher intelligence than that of science. It allows for scientific thought, encircles it, and passes infinitely beyond it. Metaphysical need is not sated through thinking about immediate causes and their intermediary stages; it can only find complete satisfaction by going back to the beginning of beginnings, which explains all and which nothing can entirely explain. The finite is marked out in a corner of the infinite.

Beyond certain limits, therefore, one should not marvel at the works of man or the works of nature, however magnificent they may be. The power through which the magician acts, limited as it is in time, space and effects, is only a borrowed power, always subject to withdrawal by the Lender:

> *... There is no power save in Allāh ...*
>
> 18:39

> *... Thee do we beseech for help.*
>
> 1:4

We have not properly understood the Qur'an if we interpret otherwise the systematic refusal on the part of the Prophet to pass himself off as a maker of miracles. Some have insinuated from this that he was not given any signs of the divinity of his mission. Was it then arbitrarily, and without any proof, that he imposed belief in his mission on mankind? Would that not be the ultimate folly, or as good as?

The truth is that, in all the extraordinary circumstances which surround prophets, establish their missions and assure their success, Qur'anic doctrine never sees any action as purely and simply human. It is by the power of God that such and such a marvel was accomplished by the lips or hands of His apostles. They had no more right, nor choice, than those to whom they preached to demand such an exchange of power. Noah and the former prophets had already proclaimed this:

> *... Only Allāh will bring it on you, if He please ...*
>
> 11:33

> *... And it is not for us to bring you an authority, except by Allāh's permission ...*
>
> 14:11

And when the Pharisees asked him to make them a sign in the sky, what else could Jesus do but decline their request and go away?[3]

God gives his credentials to whom He will, in the form that He wishes and judges to be the most appropriate, in order to persuade the people of such and such an era in history and such and such an epoch of humanity. Moses throws his staff, and behold, to his surprise, it is transformed into *a serpent, gliding*.[4] Jesus calls the dead man, and by the authority of God the dead man comes to life:[5]

> *... and when thou didst raise the dead by My permission ...*
>
> 5:110

It happened in the same way for Muhammad, when the recitation of some verses disarmed the most ferocious rebels and made them pass from spiritual death to life:

> *O you who believe, respond to Allāh and His Messenger, when he calls you to that which gives you life. And know that Allāh comes in between a man and his heart, and that to Him you will be gathered.*
>
> 8:24

It is not Muhammad who opens closed hearts, nor is it he who makes the deaf hear and the blind see:

> *So surely thou canst not make the dead to hear, nor canst thou make the deaf to hear the call ... Nor canst thou guide the blind out of their error ...*
>
> 30:52-3

It is by the will of God that all these benefits are accomplished:

> *Surely thou canst not guide whom thou lovest, but Allāh guides whom He pleases ...*
>
> 28:56

> *Is he who was dead, then We raised him to life and made for him a light by which he walks among the people, like him whose likeness is that of one in darkness whence he cannot come forth? ...*
>
> 6:123

So whomsoever Allāh intends to guide, He expands his breast for Islam, and whomsoever He intends to leave in error, he makes his breast strait (and) narrow as though he were ascending upwards ...

6:126

For everything depends absolutely on Him:

... nay, the commandment is wholly Allāh's. Do not those who believe know that, if Allāh please, He would certainly guide all the people? ...

13:31

When a divided society, long consumed by hate and internal wars, overnight became a closely bonded group of intimate friends, such an abrupt mutation of souls was not due to the action of a man. Indeed, it could not be achieved by all the terrestrial forces serried together; only God has power over hearts and is able to unite them:

And He has united their hearts. If thou hadst spent all that is in the earth, thou couldst not have united their hearts, but Allāh united them ...

8:63

... And remember Allāh's favour to you when you were enemies, then He united your hearts so by His favour you became brethren ...

3:102

When faith finally triumphed over infidelity, and the weaker group overcame the stronger, this was scarcely due to the heroic deeds of the Prophet or the courage of the individual faithful: it was God Himself who killed the adversary :

So you slew them not but Allāh slew them ...

8:17

From one end of the Qur'an to the other, one finds the same explanation for the miracles performed through the intermission of prophets, Muhammad as much as the others. Whether a story from earlier days:

These are announcements relating to the unseen which We reveal to thee; thou didst not know them – (neither) thou nor thy people – before this.

11:49

This is of the announcements relating to the unseen (which) We reveal to thee, and thou wast not with them when they resolved upon their affair, and they were devising plans.

12:102

And thou wast not on the western side when We revealed to Moses the commandment, nor wast thou among those present; ... And thou wast not dwelling among the people of Midian ...

28:44-6

or a prediction for the future:

The Romans are vanquished in a near land, and they, after their defeat, will gain victory.

30:2-3

or the unveiling of the secret of a trial in order to find the most just formula by which to judge it:

Allāh has ... taught thee what thou knewest not ...

4:113

These are thanks neither to the perspicacity of a prophet's intelligence:

... So when he told her of it, she said: Who informed thee of this? He said: The Knowing, the One Aware, informed me.

66:3

nor the breadth of his mortal education. They are simply a result of the intervention of Mercy, from which all creation, all knowledge and all goodness proceed.

Through the idea of the potency of the Divine Attributes the Qur'an thus establishes the first part of its communal religious doctrine, there is only one object worthy of our adoration, and goes on to construct the second – the doctrine of the future life. God is not only the beginning, He is also the end:

He is the First and the Last ...

57:3

It is to Him that we shall return:

How can you deny Allāh and you were without life and He gave you life? Again, He will cause you to die and again bring you to life, then you shall be brought back to Him.

2:28

in order to render an account of our deeds and receive retribution according to our deserts:

> *And guard yourselves against a day in which you will be returned to Allāh. Then every soul will be paid in full what it has earned, and they will not be wronged.*
>
> 2:281

Here it is necessary to distinguish between two points: the survival of the soul and the resurrection of the body. As far as the former is concerned, it does not seem that the preaching of Islam met any considerable opposition. The Qur'an, which records with extreme fidelity all the objections raised by its adversaries, only mentions one incident. The pagan Arabs already had a vague, if rather superstitious, idea of some kind of life of the soul after death. Pre-Islamic poetry gives us to understand that their thirst for vengeance led them to believe in a fabulous entity which they called Hāma. This kind of double floated at night above its victim's sepulchre, crying, 'Give me to drink!' It kept on reappearing and imploring until satisfaction was extracted for the crime perpetrated upon it. Prophetic tradition denied the existence of such an entity, thereby confirming to us that it was indeed prevalent in pre-Islamic society.

It was against the second proposition that the impious heaped their objections and their sarcasm. Sceptics, too attached to their own everyday experiences, did not find it easy to believe that a completely dissolved human corpse could once again take on its integral form and begin to live again. *When we are bones and decayed particles,* said the incredulous, *shall we then be raised up as a new creation?*[6] They declared that whoever maintained such an assertion either had *madness in him* or had *forged a lie against Allāh.*[7] *So bring our fathers (back), if you are truthful.*[8] *There is naught but our first death and we shall not be raised again.*[9]

The Qur'an has a decisive argument against these facile reasonings, elicited from the book of nature. It displays for us a thousand pictures in which the magnificent power of God is manifested: God has drawn men from the earth; to her He makes them return; from her He will make them arise a second time:

> *From it We created you, and into it We shall return you, and from it raise you back a second time.*
>
> 20:55

Let anyone meditate a little on the successive forms that a human being takes (and He created you in stages), from the first cluster of cells to the marvellous form in which man is born:

> *And certainly We create man of an extract of clay, then We make him a small life-germ in a firm resting-place, then We make the life-germ a clot, then We make the clot a lump of flesh, then We make (in) the lump of flesh bones, then We clothe the bones with flesh, then We cause it to grow into another creation ... then after that you certainly die.*
>
> 23:12-16

> *He brings forth the living from the dead and brings forth the dead from the living, and gives life to the earth after its death. And thus will you be brought forth.*
>
> 30:19

Would it not be easy for the Artisan who wrought the first creation to recreate it?:

> *And He it is, Who originates the creation, then reproduces it, and it is very easy to Him ...*
>
> 30:27

The Qur'an particularly draws our attention towards the seasons. Do we not see how the earth, from being dry and sterile, becomes fertile?:

> *O people, if you are in doubt about the Resurrection, then surely We created you from dust, then from a small life-germ, then from a clot, then from a lump of flesh, complete in make and incomplete, that We may make clear to you. And We cause what We please to remain in the wombs till an appointed time, then We bring you forth as babies then that you may attain your maturity. And of you is he who is caused to die, and of you is he who is brought back to the worst part of life, so that after knowledge he knows nothing. And thou seest the earth barren, but when We send down thereon water, it stirs and swells and brings forth a beautiful (growth) of every kind. That is because Allāh, He is the Truth, and He gives life to the dead, and He is Possessor of power over all things.*
>
> 22:5-6

> *Look then at the signs of Allāh's mercy, how He gives life to the earth after its death. Surely He is the Quickener of the dead; and He is possessor of power over all things.*
>
> 30:50

The sceptics will admit the possibility of new vegetal life, but say, how can human life return after senses and consciousness have been severed from the body? Yet he who reasons thus has only to refer to the everyday alternation of sleep and waking. This offers us a kind of insight into the succession of life and death:

> *And He it is Who takes your souls at night, and He knows what you earn by day, then He raises you up therein that an appointed term may be fulfilled. Then to Him is your return, then He will inform you of what you did.*
>
> 6:60

> *Allāh takes (men's) souls at the time of their death, and those that die not, during their sleep. Then He withholds those on whom He has passed the decree of death and sends the others back till an appointed time.*
>
> 39:42

It is not therefore impossible, indeed it is strongly probable, that we shall have another life. On what can we base our certitude? The Qur'an. It not only shows us that this is Divine Decree, an obligation which God has imposed upon Himself:

> *And they swear by Allāh their most energetic oaths: Allāh will not raise up him who dies. Yea! it is a promise binding on Him, quite true, but most people know not.*
>
> 16:38

but also one of the demands of supreme justice and the highest wisdom:

> *So that He might make manifest to them that about which they differ ...*
>
> 16:39

> *... that every soul may be rewarded for what it has earned ...*
>
> 45:22

> *Do you then think that We have created you in vain, and that you will not be returned to us?*
>
> 23:115

> *Does man think that he will be left aimless?*
>
> 75:36

The two great propositions of the one and only religion which the Qur'an aims to re-establish are thus either truths already recognizable in themselves, or founded on self-evident principles. For a theoretical demonstration one could not ask for a more pressing form of persuasion.

Even if this religious theme remains fundamentally unchanged, it has no less undergone real progress in order to assume its Qur'anic form. The Qur'an does not only administer its proofs in a manner to convince the most demanding spirits and make the hardest hearts vibrate, stretch its perspectives far and deep across the whole of the universe, celestial and terrestrial, and draw its lessons from every aspect of creation, internal and external.

The religious material itself, concerning the attributes of God and the destiny of the soul, is more developed here than in any other source. There is a quite particular purity which characterizes the sense of the Divine manifested in the Qur'an, distancing it from that materialistic anthropomorphism into which the human imagination so easily falls. Finally there is the pervasive power which deflects the listener from his material cares, however strong they may be, and transports him or her, in one step, to the sublime realm of the spirit.[10]

5
Goodness, or the Moral Element

But the human soul is not nourished by theoretical truths alone. Man does not only require knowledge and belief; he demands a practical regimen, one that can direct his activities from moment to moment, in his personal behaviour, in his relationships with others, and in his dealings with God. The final revelation provides this in the most detailed and precise manner, tracing a determinable path for each branch of human activity.

It is not enough for a true believer to have an unshakeable faith in revealed truths. One must also put oneself at the service of this faith, making a gift of oneself and one's property:

> *The believers are those only who believe in Allāh and His Messenger, then they doubt not, and struggle hard with their wealth and their lives in the way of Allāh. Such are the truthful ones.*
>
> 49:15

One must accomplish one's duty as a good believer and a good citizen, that is to say adore God and do good:

> *They only are believers whose hearts are full of fear when Allāh is mentioned, and when His messages are recited to them they increase them in faith, and in their Lord do they trust, those who keep up prayer and spend out of what We have given them.*
>
> 8:2-3

> *O you who believe, bow down and prostrate yourselves and serve your Lord, and do good that you may succeed.*
>
> 22:77

Religion is dogma and law, belief and obedience:

> *The Messenger believes in what has been revealed to him from his Lord, and (so do) the believers. They all believe in Allāh and His angels and His Books and His messengers. We make no difference between any of His messengers. And they say: We hear and obey ...*
>
> 2:285

To believe in transcendent truths and practise both personal and altruistic virtues – this is the Qur'anic definition of goodness, in the full sense of the word:

> *It is not righteousness that you turn your faces towards the East and the West, but righteous is the one who believes in Allāh, and the Last Day, and the angels, and the Book and the prophets, and gives away wealth out of love for Him to the near of kin and the orphans and the needy and the wayfarer and to those who ask and to set slaves free and keeps up prayer and pays the poor-rate: and the performers of their promise when they make a promise, and the patient in distress and affliction and in the time of conflict. These are they who are truthful; and these are they who keep their duty.*
>
> 2:177

Practical matters have great importance in the Qur'an; they feature frequently and quite explicitly as a necessary condition for final salvation and eternal happiness. Even where the Qur'an does not mention them in the text, it is not difficult to imply their presence from the term *mu'min* (believer), according to the definitions just cited.

Does this dual requirement not call for a certain order of precedence between the two aspects? Hardly anyone would deny that the possession of faith constitutes a sine qua non of salvation, but does the same apply to observation of the law, and if so, up to what point?

Is a grave sin which is not repented of before death absolutely unpardonable? Put another way, does such a sin irrevocably mean eternal damnation (as the majority of Muʿtazilites believe) or temporary punishment (as some Muʿtazilites believe); does the faith of the sinner, through the mercy of God, automatically re-establish him (as pure Murji'ites believe);[1] has God the right to absolve certain sins for certain of the faithful in certain conditions, without us ourselves being able to say which they should be (the Ashʿarites' belief)?

Yet such a theological discussion, which bears on the secondary and negative aspects of the problem – degree, duration, the certitude of Divine chastisement for such and such a fault – leaves out not only moral and social responsibility, but also, more importantly, the positive value of virtuous action. It is by progress towards virtue that one ascends the scale of merit:

> *And for all are degrees according to what they do, and that He may pay them for their deeds and they will not be wronged.*
>
> 46:19

We do not intend to enumerate here the assemblage of precepts which together make up the practical wisdom of the Qur'an;[2] that would take us outside the restricted terms of reference of this work. We shall content ourselves rather with indicating certain aspects by which this teaching must have taken hold of men's souls, as much by the material and content of the doctrine as by the fashion in which it is presented.

Firstly the method.

Within each of us lies an innate moralist. However great the failings and corruption into which we can fall, apart from in exceptional instances of errors of conscience, we recognize, love and admire virtue per se in others, even when we do not have the courage to elevate ourselves to that same level. Though we ourselves may be drawn to do the very thing we reproach in others, the spectacle of an unworthy attitude fills us with repugnance. We hate our faults and, if we do not make a constant effort to correct them, always try to exonerate ourselves. What man enjoys being considered a liar, hypocrite, coward, trickster, drunkard, or such like?

It is upon this more or less universal feeling for the just and the unjust, the good and the bad, that the Qur'an most often leans in its teaching and when defining its practical doctrine. Here, then, are certain formulae which the Qur'an uses to summarize and synthesize its moral message: the Prophet, it says, *enjoins them good and forbids them evil, and makes lawful to them the good things and prohibits for them impure things;*[3] *Allāh enjoins justice and the doing of good (to others) and the giving to the kindred and He forbids indecency and evil and rebellion;*[4] *Allāh enjoins not indecency;*[5] *My Lord forbids only indecencies, such of them as are apparent and such as are concealed, and sin and unjust rebellion.*[6]

Rather than continuing with a string of citations, let it suffice that we note that there are more than forty-five references in the Qur'an to a universal moral conscience and to man's innate feeling for good and evil.[7]

Since this natural sentiment is not always sufficiently awakened to ensure universal submission to the rule, however, a complete method of education cannot rest there. A careful teacher, wanting to make quite sure of the efficacy of his instruction, must have recourse to another, no less powerful way, independent of our individual consent.

Parallel to the moral sense and beyond it, the human soul is endowed with intelligence and reason. Thus, in the absence of a vivid sense of good and evil, there is always the concept of mutual duty, universally recognized as such. The best means of awakening this concept, and of enabling it to transcend opposing feelings, is to invoke in its support competent recommendations – from wise men and saints of all generations.

Accordingly, a theme very dear to the final revelation is its linkage in one body with the revelations which preceded it, its function in rekindling a light which had over the centuries become pale. The principal duties of the science of truth are presented by the Qur'an as having been preached already to the ancients.

Thus, all the messengers of God held up the scales of justice:

> *Certainly We sent Our messengers with clear arguments, and sent down with them the Book and the measure, that men may conduct themselves with equity ...*
>
> 57:25

and all received the command to earn their living with honour, to worship God and to practise virtue:

> *O ye messengers, eat of the good things and do good ...*
>
> 23:51

Prayer and the giving of alms were instituted by Abraham, Isaac, Jacob:

> *We revealed to them the doing of good and the keeping up of prayer and the giving of alms ...*
>
> 21:73

Ismāʿīl:

> *And he enjoined on his people prayer and almsgiving ...*
>
> 19:55

Moses:

> *... serve Me, and keep up prayer for My remembrance.*
>
> 20:14

and Jesus:

> *... He has enjoined on me prayer and poor-rate so long as I live.*
>
> 19:31

Fasting was equally prescribed to earlier peoples:

O you who believe, fasting is prescribed for you, as it was prescribed for those before you, so that you may guard against evil.

2:183

while pilgrimage was first established by Abraham:

And proclaim to men the Pilgrimage ...

22:27

All the nations had their sacred rites:

And for every nation We appointed acts of devotion ...

22:34

To every nation We appointed acts of devotion, which they observe ...

22:67

Materialism, excessive love of the world, aggression and corruption were condemned by Hūd and Sāliḥ:

Do you build on every height a monument? You (only) sport.

26:128

Lot rose up against the debauchery of his people:

And obey not the bidding of the extravagant, who make mischief in the land and act not aright.

26:151-2

Do you come to the males from among the creatures, and leave your wives whom your Lord has created for you? Nay, you are a people exceeding limits.

26:165-6

Shuʿayb against fraudulent commercial dealings:

Give full measure and be not of those who diminish. And weigh with a true balance.

26:181-2

The sage Luqmān vividly advised his son to exhort others to goodness and prevent them from committing evil, while at the same time enduring the hardships which would ensue from such a noble task. He enjoined gentleness and modesty upon him:

> *O my son, keep up prayer and enjoin good and forbid evil, and bear patiently that which befalls thee. Surely this is an affair of great resolution. And turn not thy face away from people in contempt, nor go about the land exultingly. Surely Allāh loves not any self-conceited boaster. And pursue the right course in thy going about and lower thy voice …*
>
> 31:17-19

It is not by chance that Muhammad teaches the same law as his predecessors. The Qur'an lays this out in its address to the Muslims:

> *Allāh desires to explain to you, and to guide you in the ways of those before you …*
>
> 4:26

and in addressing the Prophet himself; having enumerated his predecessors, the Divine messengers, it says:

> *These are they whom Allāh guided, so follow their guidance …*
>
> 6:91

Indeed, we do not find a single moral precept reported in the Qur'an as having being taught by a previous prophet or sage, which is not then taken up as a duty for the Muslim community.

So you want to extract from the Qur'an the moral laws of Moses and Jesus as rendered in the Holy Bible? You will find them, precisely conserved, every nuance of style retained. To be sure, they are not given *en bloc* as they are in the Ten Commandments or the Sermon on the Mount, but they are present, distributed throughout the various Meccan and Medinan chapters. For the most part, they are each given in the context of a sentence intended to judge a given situation.

Apart from the choice of Sabbath day, which the Qur'an considers a local and conditional duty, the Qur'an confirms the Ten Commandments:

The Pentateuch	The Qur'an
You shall have no other gods.	And thy Lord has decreed that you serve none but Him … 17:23 (among other passages)

You shall not prostrate before any graven image.	… Shun the filth of idols … 22:30
You shall not take the name of thy Lord God in vain.	… He will call you to account for the making of deliberate oaths … 5:89
	Make not Allāh by your oaths … 2:224
Honour thy father and thy mother.	… do good to parents … 17:23
Thou shalt not kill.	… and kill not your people … 4:29
Thou shalt not commit adultery.	Say to the believing men that they lower their gaze and restrain their sexual passions … and say to the believing women that they lower their gaze and restrain their sexual passions … 24:30-1
Thou shalt not steal.	And (as for) the man and the woman addicted to theft, cut off their hands 5:38
	… a pledge that they … will not steal 60:12
Thou shalt not bear false witness against thy neighbour.	… and shun false words. 22:30
Thou shalt not covet another man's property.	And covet not that by which Allāh has made some of you excel others 4:32

These are the foundations of the moral law, of which Jesus was to say that he who suppressed the least important of the Commandments would be the least important in the kingdom of heaven, yet he who observed them and taught them to others would be called great in the kingdom of heaven.

But it would be an under-estimation of Moses' work to reduce it to these elementary duties. If we look deeper into the Torah, we find other commandments, scattered between Exodus 22-3, Leviticus 19-25 and Deuteronomy 6. These take into consideration acts of heart as much as exterior deeds, and anticipate the precepts of the Gospel:

The Pentateuch	The Qur'an
Thou shalt not spread false rumours, or calumny.	Those who love that scandal should circulate respecting those who believe, for them is a grievous chastisement in this world and the Hereafter … 24:19
	… [do not] let some of you backbite others … 49:12
Thou shalt not join with the wicked to do evil.	… help not one another in sin and aggression … 5:2
Thou shalt not favour the poor in a court case.	O you who believe, be maintainers of justice, bearers of witness for Allāh, even though it be against your own selves or (your) parents or near relatives – whether he be rich or poor 4:135
You should help your neighbour.	… help one another in righteousness and piety … 5:2
You should treat the stranger amongst you as one of your own people.	… be good to the parents and to the near of kin and the orphans and the needy and the neighbour of (your) kin and the alien neighbour, and the companion in a journey and the wayfarer and those whom your right hands possess [slaves] … 4:36
You will uphold the poor, brother or stranger, who hold out their hands.	Who are constant at their prayer, and in whose wealth there is a known right for the beggar and the destitute. 70:23-5
Thou shalt not oppress the stranger or foreigner.	As above. 4:36
Thou shalt not afflict orphaned girls or boys.	… Allāh makes known to you His decision concerning … the weak among children, and that you should

	deal justly with orphans … 4:127
	Therefore the orphan, oppress not. 93:9
Thou shalt not give false judgement.	… when you judge between people … judge with justice … 4:58
Thou shalt neither lie nor deceive.	… shun false words. 22:30
	… Surely Allāh loves not him who is treacherous, sinful. 4:107
Thou shalt not take revenge.	… those who restrain their anger and pardon men … 3:133
Thou shalt not give short measure.	Woe to the cheaters! Who … when they measure out to others or weigh out for them, they give less than is due. 83:1-3
Thou shalt not bear any malice against the children of your people.	… forgive us and our brethren who had precedence of us in faith, and leave no spite in our hearts towards those who believe … 59:10
Be holy, saintly.	… Be worshippers of the Lord … 3:78
	… In [the mosque] are men who love to purify themselves. And Allāh loves those who purify themselves. 9:108
Thou shalt love thy neighbour as thyself.	… [they] love those who have fled to them … and prefer (them) before themselves, though poverty may afflict them … 59:9

Thou shalt love God with all thy heart.

Yet there are some men who take for themselves objects of worship besides Allāh, whom they love as they should love Allāh. And those who believe are stronger in (their) love for Allāh …

2:165

The most profound and most elevated teaching, however, is to be found in the Sermon on the Mount: a veritable moral treasure which is of inestimable value. Now, here again, the Qur'an acquits itself marvellously of its prime mission as faithful guardian of all the sacred Books:

And We have revealed to thee the Book with the truth, verifying that which is before it of the Book and a guardian over it …

5:48

Still faithful to its favourite method, rather than accumulating all the advice in one place, the Qur'an prefers more often to point out each lesson as it arises. Let us follow step by step the evangelical sermon and see how the principles in it are confirmed in the holy Book of Islam.

The Gospel	The Qur'an
Blessed are the poor in spirit: for theirs is the kingdom of heaven.	The life of this world is made to seem fair to those who disbelieve, and they mock those who believe. And those who keep their duty are above them on the day of Resurrection … 2:212
	Fair-seeming to men is made the love of desires, of women and sons and hoarded treasures of gold and silver and well-bred horses and cattle and tilth. This is the provision of the life of this world. And Allāh – with Him is the good goal (of life). 3:13
Blessed are they that mourn, for they shall be comforted.	And We shall certainly try you with something of fear and hunger and loss of property and lives and fruits. And give good news to the patient. 2:155

Blessed are the meek, for they shall inherit the earth.

And hasten to forgiveness from your Lord and a Garden, as wide as the heavens and the earth; it is prepared for those who keep their duty … and those who restrain (their) anger and pardon men …

3:132-3

Blessed are they which do hunger and thirst after righteousness, for they shall be filled.

Or do those who do evil deeds think that We shall make them as those who believe and do good – their life and their death being equal? Evil is what they judge!

45:21

Surely they who are guilty used to laugh at those who believe … Surely the disbelievers are rewarded as they did.

83:29-36

Blessed are the merciful, for they shall obtain mercy.

Then he is of those who … exhort one another to patience, and exhort one another to mercy. These are the people of the right hand.

90:17-18

Blessed are the pure in heart, for they shall see God.

Save him who comes to Allāh with a sound heart.

26:89

Whoever fears the Beneficent in secret, and comes with a penitent heart: Enter [Paradise] in peace …

50:33-4

Blessed are the peacemakers, for they shall be called the children of God.

There is no good in most of their secret counsels except (in) him who enjoins charity or goodness or reconciliation between people …

4:114

Blessed are they which are persecuted for righteousness' sake, for theirs is the kingdom of heaven.

Or do you think that you will enter the Garden, while there has not yet befallen you the like of what befell those who have passed away before you. Distress and affliction befell them and they were shaken violently, so that the Messenger and those who believed with him said: When will the help of Allāh come? Now surely the help of Allāh is nigh!

2:214

You will certainly be tried through your property and your persons … And if you are patient and keep your duty, surely this is an affair of great resolution.

3:185

Let us take our comparison further. When Jesus affirmed that he came not to abolish, but to confirm the law, he spoke truth indeed. And when he said, 'You have learned that the following was said to the ancients … but I say this to you …' he must have meant to imply that he was continuing a process of moral purification already begun, but with space for development and improvement:

The Gospel	The Qur'an
But I say to you that whosoever is angry with his brother without a cause shall be in danger of the judgement: and whosoever shall say to his brother, 'Raca' shall be in danger of the council: but whosoever shall say, 'Thou fool' shall be in danger of hell fire.	… and those who restrain (their) anger … 3:133 … and whenever they are angry they forgive. 42:37
Leave there thy gift before the altar, and go thy way; first be reconciled to thy brother, and then come and offer thy gift.	The believers are brothers, so make peace between your brethren … 49:10 … So keep your duty to Allāh and set aright your differences … 8:1 And relate to them with truth the story of the two sons of Adam, when they offered an offering, but it was accepted from one of them and was not accepted from the other. He said:

	I will certainly kill thee. (The other) said: Allāh accepts only from the dutiful. 5:27
But I say unto you that whosoever looketh on a woman to lust after her hath committed adultery with her already in her heart.	Say to the believing men that they lower their gaze and restrain their sexual passions … and say to the believing women that they lower their gaze and restrain their sexual passions … 24:30-1
And again, ye have heard that it hath been said by them of old time, 'Thou shalt not forswear thyself … ' … But I say unto you, 'Swear not at all … but let your communication be Yea, yea; Nay, nay …	And make not Allāh by your oaths … 2:224
You have heard that it hath been said, 'Thou shalt love thy neighbour, and hate thine enemy.' But I say unto you, 'Love your enemies … '	Lo! You are they who will love them while they love you not … 3:118
… do good to them that hate you, and pray for them which despitefully use you and persecute you.	And those who are steadfast seeking the pleasure of their Lord, and keep up prayer and spend of that which We have given them, secretly and openly, and repel evil with good … 13:22 … Repel (evil) with what is best … 41:34
And if ye salute your brethren only, what do ye more than others?	… when the ignorant address them, they say, Peace! 25:63
	Allāh forbids you not respecting those who fight you not for religion, nor drive you forth from your homes, that you show them kindness and deal with them justly … 60:8

Give to him that asketh thee, and from him that would borrow of thee turn not thou away.	… and gives away wealth … 2:177
Take heed that ye do not your alms before men, to be seen of them.	Who (do) good to be seen. 107:6
Pardon people their offences, for your celestial Father will pardon thee.	If you … pardon an evil, Allāh surely is ever Pardoning, Powerful. 4:149
	They who pardon and overlook … 24:22
Lay not up for yourselves treasures upon earth.	And you love wealth with exceeding love. 89:20
But lay up for yourselves treasures in heaven …	Whoso desires the tilth of the Hereafter, We give him increase in his tilth … 42:20
No man can serve two masters: for either he will hate the one, and love the other; or else he will hold to the one and despise the other.	Allāh sets forth a parable: A man belonging to partners differing with one another, and a man (devoted) wholly to one man. Are the two alike in condition? … 39:29
Take no thought for your life, what ye shall eat, or what ye shall drink; nor yet for your body, what ye shall put on … behold the fowls of the air: for they sow not, neither do they reap	And many a living creature carries not its sustenance! Allāh sustains it and yourselves … 29:60
Judge not, that ye be not judged … and why beholdest thou the mote that is in thy brother's eye, but considerest not the beam that is in thine own eye?	O you who believe, let not people laugh at people, perchance they may be better than they; nor let women (laugh) at women, perchance they may be better than they … 49:11
Give not that which is holy unto the dogs.	And remind, for reminding profits the believer. 51:55
Ask, and it shall be given you.	And when My servants ask thee

	concerning Me, surely I am nigh. I answer the prayer of the suppliant when he calls on Me … 2:186
	And your Lord says: Pray to Me, I will answer you … 40:60
Therefore all things whatsoever ye would that men should do to you, do ye even so to them …	… aim not at the bad to spend thereof, while you would not take it yourselves unless you connive at it 2:267
	And let those fear who, should they leave behind them weakly offspring, would fear on their account; so let them observe their duty to Allāh and let them speak right words. 4:9
Enter ye in at the strait gate …	But he attempts not the uphill road; and what will make thee comprehend what the uphill road is? 90:11-12
Beware of false prophets, which come to you in sheep's clothing, but inwardly they are ravening wolves.	And of men is he whose speech about the life of this world pleases thee, and he calls Allāh to witness as to that which is in his heart, yet he is the most violent of adversaries. 2:204

In the course of this enumeration, we have omitted two articles of the New Testament which seem to contradict the law of Moses. These concern divorce and retaliation.

The Pentateuch appears to grant unbridled freedom to a husband who wishes to repudiate his wife, on account of his finding something shameful in her, or his feeling an aversion towards her. Yet the Gospel seems to support the indissolubility of marriage, except in cases of infidelity. Similarly, in sharp contrast to the Pentateuch's implacable demand for a murderer's blood and for like reparation in return for every offence, are Jesus' teachings concerning the duty of forgiveness and not resisting the wicked. If we look at the letter of the law, then, Christianity would appear to abolish laws which it recognizes as having been previously established.

But if we look at matters more closely, we see that we have here nothing more than two aspects, or two degrees, of one and the same eternal law, one of whose poles is justice, and the other charity. Morality oscillates between these two limits, unable to restrict itself to just one at the expense of the other, or to escape its alternative.

To the person who wishes to exercise his rights, justice accords certain human conditions beyond which one cannot pass; but there is no reproach for the one who wishes generously to waive his due. Charity invites us to such acts of generosity, though it does not of course mean to condone crime or encourage vice. To disregard the possibility of making a benevolent gesture is to lack moral sensibility, yet to make such a gesture at the expense of other, more essential principles, is nonsensical. One has to decide according to the merits and defects of the case, much as one's treatment of a malady – by normal, moderate means, with delicacy and circumspection, or using some more severe method – depends upon the gravity of the illness and the condition of the patient.

In our opinion, one either has to mutually recognize and understand the two sets of formulae from the Old and New Testaments in their alternation, or admit that neither formula could stand independently, except for within a restricted group of humanity or over a limited period in history. Now, while proposing as an ideal model the indissoluble unity of our very first ancestors, the Gospel seems to admit, we believe, the hard reality of those who do not know how to settle things otherwise:[8]

> He saith unto them, 'Moses because of the hardness of your hearts suffered you to put away your wives: but from the beginning it was not so.'
>
> Matt. 19:8-11

The Torah, meanwhile, though it usually claims life for life and wound for wound, often urges us to content ourselves with apprehending the offender, and not pursue vengeance on our neighbour.[9] Thus the two holy Books would appear to have each retained one half of the true moral formula, leaving the other more or less implicit.

The Qur'an takes it upon itself to give the entire formula as explicitly as possible, without, however, forgetting to indicate the respective value of the two poles:

> *And if you take your turn, then punish with the like of that with which you were afflicted. But if you show patience, it is certainly best for the patient.*
>
> 16:126

So much for retribution, then, and forgiveness. As to the right of divorce, the Qur'an explains what hurdles a man has to pass before he can think of breaking this sacred union:

> *And if you wish to have (one) wife in the place of another and you have given one of them a heap of gold, take nothing from it ... how can you take it when one of you has already gone in to the other and they have taken from you a strong covenant?*
>
> 4:20-1

> *And if a woman fears ill-usage from her husband or desertion no blame is on them if they effect a reconciliation between them. And reconciliation is better ...*
>
> 4:128

> *And if you fear a breach between the two, appoint an arbiter from his people and an arbiter from her people ...*
>
> 4:35

We need to read further to find out how many attempts at reconciliation are necessary before a break can become final:

> *And the divorced women should keep themselves in waiting for three courses. And it is not lawful for them to conceal that which Allāh has created in their wombs, if they believe in Allāh and the Last Day. And their husbands have a better right to take them back in the meanwhile if they wish for reconciliation. And women have rights similar to those against them in a just manner, and men are a degree above them ... Divorce may be (pronounced) twice; then keep (them) in good fellowship or let (them) go with kindness. And it is not lawful for you to take any part of what you have given them ...*
>
> 2:228-30

> *O Prophet, when you divorce women, divorce them for their prescribed period, and calculate the period; and keep your duty to Allāh, your Lord. Turn them not out of their houses – nor should they themselves go forth – unless they commit an open indecency. And these are the limits of Allāh. And whoever goes beyond the limits of Allāh, he indeed wrongs his own soul. Thou knowest not that Allāh may after that bring about an event. So when they have reached their prescribed time, retain them with kindness or dismiss them with kindness, and call to witness two just ones from among you, and give upright testimony for Allāh ...*
>
> 65:1-2

In the end, however, doesn't someone who revokes a decision to separate thereby efface his fault and bring Divine mercy down upon him?:

> *... then if they do go back, Allāh is surely Forgiving, Merciful.*
>
> 2:226

In Islam, then, divorce cannot be considered an ambivalent act, or one that is absolutely permitted; the Prophet said, 'Among allowable things, the act which God detests the most is the breaking up of a marriage.'[10]

Thus the Qur'an explains and justifies the prophets by bringing together and synthesizing their Works. In this unification of diversity, and in this admission of varying degrees of merit to the very heart of moral law, we believe we find one of the factors by which Islamic doctrine has been able to extend itself through such a considerable part of humanity. Islam shelters under one orthodoxy a diversity of thoughts, tendencies and natures, which could not have been satisfied either by abstract, intransigent rigour nor by an excessively inert tolerance.

In mentioning the Qur'an's conciliatory methods, we broach the object which is at the heart of its teaching. It is already remarkable for a work of morality to gather together the wisdom of the ancients, and to present a variety of lessons, disparate in age and sentiment, under the same light and such that they appear to converge towards the same goal. But the Qur'an does not stop there.

The Qur'an's first aim is to safeguard and consolidate the moral patrimony bequeathed by former revelations. It does, however, have another mission, no less precious. In the words of the Prophet, it has to complete, to finish off, and to crown the Divine edifice raised piece by piece by the prophets before him.[11] In the words of the Qur'an itself, it has to show man how he should behave:

> *Surely this Qur'ān guides to that which is most upright, and gives good news to the believers who do good that theirs is a great reward.*
>
> 17:9

What then is new and progressive in the moral teaching of the Qur'an? This can be gleaned from several brief remarks which strike the very soul of an objective reader:

1) personal virtue

On the individual moral plane, the Qur'an gives us at least one new precept and one new principle. The precept is the abolition of alcohol and the suppression of any intoxicating liquor:

O you who believe, intoxicants and games of chance and (sacrificing to) stones set up and (dividing by) arrows are only an uncleanness, the devil's work; so shun it that you may succeed. The devil desires only to create enmity and hatred among you by means of intoxicants and games of chance, and to keep you back from the remembrance of Allāh and from prayer. Will you then keep back?

5:90-1

The principle, which we would like to underline here, concerns moral intention.

In order to exhort his people, Moses made a vision flash before their eyes; an extended view of the Promised Land, victory over their enemies, blessing and abundance in all the domains of life around them. The coming of Christ then marked a new era in the teaching. In the Gospel, the promised happiness will barely take place in this world at all. The soul's sights should from now on be turned away from the terrestrial world and raised towards heaven.

Thus, using methods which are always constructive, never destructive, the Qur'an arrives at the crux of the matter: both promises, though solidly maintained, are no longer presented as motives for action. The virtuous man's goal should neither be the kingdom of heaven, nor the present world; it should be ultimate Goodness, for one can go no higher. It is God Himself Whom one should have in view when accomplishing His will:

... And whatever good thing you spend, it is to your good. And you spend not but to seek Allāh's pleasure. And whatever good thing you spend, it will be paid back to you in full, and you will not be wronged.

2:272

And none has with him any boon for a reward, except the seeking of the pleasure of his Lord ...

92:19-20

2) interpersonal virtue

Another new step is made concerning the moral rules which determine peer relationships. Where the precepts of the Pentateuch and the Gospel form a tree of virtue with leaves and branches, on Qur'anic terrain this ever-verdant tree flowers and bears fruit. To their treasure of justice and charity, jealously preserved in the holy Book of Islam, it adds an excellent augmentation on what one may call the 'ethical civilization'.

Thus it gives a veritable code of politeness:

And when you are greeted with a greeting, greet with one better than it, or return it ...

4:86

O you who believe, enter not houses other than your own houses, until you have asked permission and saluted their inmates. This is better for you that you may be mindful. But if you find no one therein, enter them not, until permission is given to you; and if it is said to you, Go back, then go back; this is purer for you ...

24:27-8

O you who believe, let those whom your right hands possess [slaves] *and those of you who have not attained to puberty ask permission of you three times: Before the morning prayer and when you put off your clothes for the heat of noon, and after the prayer of night. These are three times of privacy for you; besides these it is no sin for you nor for them* [to enter] ...

24:58

There is no blame on the blind man, nor any blame on the lame, nor blame on the sick, nor on yourselves that you eat in your own houses, or your fathers' houses, or your mothers' houses, or your brothers' houses, or your sisters' houses, or your paternal uncles' houses, or your paternal aunts' houses, or your maternal uncles' houses, or your maternal aunts' houses, or (houses) whereof you possess the keys, or your friends' (houses). It is no sin in you that you eat together or separately. So when you enter houses, greet your people with a salutation from Allāh, blessed (and) goodly ...

24:61

O you who believe, raise not your voices above the Prophet's voice, nor speak loudly to him as you speak loudly one to another ... Surely those who lower their voices before Allāh's Messenger are they whose hearts Allāh has proved for dutifulness. For them is forgiveness and a great reward. Those who call out to thee from behind the private apartments, most of them have no sense. And if they had patience till thou came out to them, it would be better for them ...

49:2-5

O you who believe, when you confer together in private, give not to each other counsel of sin and revolt and disobedience to the Messenger, but give to each other counsel of goodness and observance of duty ... O you who believe, when it is said to you, Make room in assemblies, make room ... And when it is said, Rise up, rise up ...

58:9-11

and discretion:

O you who believe, avoid most of suspicion, for surely suspicion in some cases is sin; and spy not nor let some of you backbite others. Does one of you like to eat the flesh of his dead brother? ...

49:12

and decency:

And say to the believing women ... they should not display their adornment except to their husbands or their fathers, or the fathers of their husbands, or their sons, or the sons of their husbands, or their brothers, or their brothers' sons, or their sisters' sons, or their women, or those whom their right hands possess [slaves], *or guileless male servants, or the children who know not women's nakedness ...*

24:31

And (as for) women past child-bearing, who hope not for marriage, it is no sin for them if they put off their clothes without displaying their adornment. And if they are modest, it is better for them ...

24:60

O wives of the Prophet, you are not like any other women. If you would keep your duty, be not soft in speech, lest he in whose heart is a disease yearn; and speak a word of goodness. And stay in your houses and display not your beauty like the displaying of the ignorance of yore; and keep up prayer, and pay the poor-rate, and obey Allāh and His Messenger ...

33:32-3

O you who believe, enter not the houses of the Prophet unless permission is given to you for a meal, not waiting for its cooking being finished – but when you are invited, enter and when you have taken food, disperse – not seeking to listen to talk. Surely this gives the Prophet trouble, but he forbears from you, and Allāh forbears not from the truth. And when you ask of them any goods, ask of them from behind a curtain. This is purer for your hearts and their hearts ...

33:53

O Prophet, tell thy wives and thy daughters and the women of believers to let down upon them their over-garments. This is more proper, so that they may be known, and not be given trouble ...

33:59

3) and 4) collective and universal virtue

A salient point of Judaic moral law is the watertight barrier set up between Israelite and non-Israelite. The benevolence encumbent upon an Israelite, if not limited to his own people, certainly does not extend beyond his own country (the stranger living alongside him):

> Unto a stranger thou mayest lend upon usury; but unto thy brother thou shalt not lend upon usury …
>
> Deut. 23:20

> Of a foreigner thou mayest exact *it again*: but *that* which is thine with thy brother thine hand shall release.
>
> Deut. 15:3

> … thou shalt not compel him [a Jew] to serve as a bondservant.
>
> Lev. 25:39

> Thou shalt not rule over him with rigour … Both thy bondmen, and thy bondmaids, which thou shalt have, *shall be* of the heathen that are round about you … Moreover, of the children of the strangers that do sojourn among you, of them shall ye buy …
>
> Lev. 25:43-5

Christian morality had the great merit of causing this barrier separating man from man to fall:

> For if ye love them which love you, what reward have ye? …
>
> Matt. 5:46

Yet, on the other hand, it does not so clearly display the social cohesion and sentiment of collective responsibility which the Hebrew texts reveal:

> And thou shalt teach them [the Commandments] diligently unto thy children
>
> Deut. 6:7

> … So shalt thou put the evil away from the midst of thee.
>
> Deut. 13:5

> Ye shall therefore keep all my statutes … that the land … spue you not out.
>
> Lev. 20:22

Christian social virtue, as presented by the Gospels, is more inter-individual than collective in the true sense of the word. In the past, community spirit had had to serve the double purpose of self-perpetuation and self-preservation, so to speak. In stretching beyond its own frontiers and desiring to embrace humanity, Christian love erased this exclusivist attitude and replaced it with a universal fraternity. It did not, however, insist hard enough on consolidating the sacred bonds of community.

Could one not, while in practical terms observing a cordial benevolence towards the world, create in the midst of this great human family another smaller family? One that would be more cohesive, and more conscious of its own formation as an ensemble of little cells making up one organism within this great body?

This happy marriage between universal virtue and collective virtue was cemented by the Qur'an. It teaches that there is fraternity in Adam in addition to fraternity in faith:

The believers are brethren ...

49:10

O mankind, surely We have created you from a male and a female, and made you tribes and families that you may know each other ...

49:13

That diversity of religious feeling in no way excuses us from being charitable and benevolent to others:

Allāh forbids you not respecting those who fight you not for religion ... that you show them kindness and deal with them justly ...

60:8

The Qur'an also teaches that wickedness in those who do not share our beliefs should not mean that we take on an aggressive attitude. Nor should it prevent us from being just:

... And let not hatred of a people – because they hindered you from the Sacred Mosque – incite you to transgress. And help one another in righteousness and piety ...

5:2

... let not hatred of a people incite you not to act equitably. Be just; that is nearer to observance of duty ...

5:8

Muslims are forbidden to lend to anyone on interest:

Those who swallow usury cannot arise except as he arises whom the devil prostrates by (his) touch. That is because they say, Trading is only like usury. And Allāh has allowed trading and forbidden usury ...

2:275

And whoever is pious and just within the community must be the same outside it:

> *... there is he who, if thou entrust him with a heap of wealth, would pay it back to thee; and among them is he who, if thou entrust him with a dīnār would not pay it back to thee, unless thou kept on demanding it. This is because they say there is no blame on us in the matter of the unlearned people and they forge a lie against Allāh while they know. Yea, whoever fulfills his promise and keeps his duty – then Allāh surely loves the dutiful.*
>
> 3:74-5

If, in certain cases, the Muslim has to have a particular reason to deliver his brothers from captivity:

> *And a believer would not kill a believer except by mistake. And he who kills a believer by mistake should free a believing slave, and blood-money should be paid to his people unless they remit it as alms ...*
>
> 4:92

in other cases, the liberation of a slave constitutes either an obligation incumbent upon him:

> *... He will call you to account for the making of deliberate oaths, so its expiation is the feeding of ten poor men with the average (food) you feed your families with, or their clothing, or the freeing of a neck ...*
>
> 5:89

or one of the most meritorious actions, which the Qur'an does not cease to eulogize:

> *... righteous is the one who ... gives away wealth ... and ... set*[s] *slaves free ...*
>
> 2:177

> *And what will make thee comprehend what the uphill road is? (It is) to free a slave.*
>
> 90:12-13

The idea of universal virtue, introduced by the Gospel, is thus extended into the varied domains of life, and accordingly developed and refined. Does this mean then that the Muslim community should let go its internal bonds in order to lose itself in a sea of humanity? On the contrary, two important commandments serve to remind the community of its role as a distinctive, organic entity.

The first enjoins believers to present themselves as an indivisible group, without schism or dissension, united around their ideal and behind their leader:

> *And hold fast by the covenant of Allāh all together and be not disunited ...*
>
> 3:102

> *O you who believe, obey Allāh and obey the Messenger and those in authority from among you ...*
>
> 4:59

> *And obey Allāh and His Messenger and dispute not one with another, lest you get weak-hearted and your power depart; and be steadfast ...*
>
> 8:46

Certain orientalists have amused themselves by depicting the Muslim as 'an intransigent individualist' who has never known 'the bond of solidarity'.[12] Thus we find, for example:[13]

> The Muslim religion respects and consecrates individualism. It knows nothing of the communion of souls in a large group. Shared actions, like the Friday prayer, the ceremony at Arafat and feast-time prayer gatherings, are individual acts accomplished by the faithful at the same time and in the same place. They are not directed, ordered or harmonised group ceremonies.

But anyone who has been present at a Muslim communal prayer gathering will realize that nothing could be more untrue. Not at all are the faithful scattered here and there in disorder, each one praying for himself, or mere spectators while the guide undertakes the essentials of the ritual task quite alone. Muslims at communal prayer are well arranged, in perfect order, tightly packed. Elbow to elbow, rich next to poor, manager cheek by jowl with his subordinate. All occupy the same position, the same direction, the same words. Each prays for all:

> *Thee do we serve and Thee do we beseech for help. Guide us on the right path.*
>
> 1:4-5

All those at prayer desire salvation, not for their present assembly alone, but for *all good servants of God*, wherever they may find themselves.

This external harmony is, without doubt, a means of bringing about an intimate communion of hearts. Islam is not just a religion; it is also a brotherhood:

The believers are brethren ...

49:10

The *ḥadīth* likens the solidarity of believers to the human body: all parts feel the pain of a single organ and work together to defend it.

After all, the two essential duties – the twin duties, as Muslims call them – whose omission calls down upon the miscreant the most severe censure, are prayer and the paying of community tax. Here, among other instances, is eloquent testimony of the spirit of solidarity in Islam.

The second commandment, which is of extreme moral importance, is the universal duty to not allow evil to triumph amongst them:

And guard yourselves against an affliction which may not smite those of you exclusively who are unjust ...

8:25

Thus they must mutually encourage each other to truth and virtue:

... exhort one another to Truth, and exhort one another to patience.

103:3

Then he is of those who believe and exhort one another to patience, and exhort one another to mercy.

90:17

To commend to his co-religionists what is right and just, and to forbid any incorrect attitude, is every Muslim's right, be he great or small; indeed it is his duty. The salvation of our fellow beings, no less than their material good, should not leave us indifferent. Together we should all collaborate in making virtue and piety reign in our midst:

... And help one another in righteousness and piety ...

5:2

The Qur'an places such value on the practice of this moral solidarity that it highlights it as the distinguishing feature of the most meritorious nation that ever existed:

You are the best nation raised up for men: you enjoin good and forbid evil and you believe in Allāh ...

3:109

5) international and inter-confessional virtue

There is another chapter in Islamic morality which is quite new to Islam. Neither Judaism nor Christianity had any occasion to undertake relations with opposing states at the time of their founders. We find Jesus' quite pacific and localized teaching on the one hand, and, in total contrast on the other, Moses' struggle against neighbouring nations which were quickly exterminated. Yet the situation was quite other for Muhammad. Over 12 years he was in constant communication with other nations and other religions. Sometimes these were hostile, sometimes peaceful.

These particular circumstances, which made of the spiritual and moral guide a diplomat and army leader, necessitated moral legislation on the conditions governing war and peace. We find the basic principles of this legislation in the Qur'an. Thus, for instance, the principle whereby legitimate war is defined as that which is undertaken in self-defence:

> *And fight in the way of Allāh against those who fight against you but be not aggressive …*
>
> 2:190

and which must cease as soon as the aggression of the enemy is ended:

> *… So if they withdraw from you and fight you not and offer you peace, then Allāh allows you no way against them.*
>
> 4:90

> *And if they incline to peace, incline thou also to it, and trust in Allāh …*
>
> 8:61

Similarly, the principle which makes any agreement sacrosanct, however unfair it may seem; a treaty that has been concluded must be loyally and piously respected, even if it is disadvantageous to the Muslims:

> *And fulfill the covenant of Allāh, when you have made a covenant, and break not the oaths after making them fast, and you have indeed made Allāh your surety. Surely Allāh knows what you do. And be not like her who unravels her yarn, disintegrating it into pieces, after she has spun it strongly …*
>
> 16:91-2

Even if an adversary begins to betray a pact, a Muslim cannot attack him deceitfully, without warning. He must first denounce the alliance in such a fashion that each is clear about where he stands:[14]

> *And if thou fear treachery on the part of a people, throw back to them (their treaty) on terms of equality. Surely Allāh loves not the treacherous.*
>
> 8:58

Further to all of this are the regulations established by *ḥadīth*. For this tide of humanity, these managed to considerably attenuate, if not eliminate, any regrettable consequences of their behaviour.

6
Beauty, or the Literary Element

As we have said before, in the depths of the human soul there exists a kind of inner viewpoint by which true can be discerned from false, and good from evil, in whatever form they present themselves, provided only that they are seen clearly and coolly.

Penetrating spirits and well-disposed souls ask no more from a new doctrine than that it should fulfill for them the double condition of teaching the truth and exhorting to virtue. Without necessarily being attracted by its outer envelope, they will quickly uncover the kernel of a new doctrine and recognize its value. The Emperor Heraclius' ignorance of the Arabic language did not prevent him from judging the Prophet's message in the light of certain moral criteria estimated by him as necessary and sufficient to establish the divinity of a mission.[1]

But it is not like this for the ordinary man. We are more attracted by charm of form than by permanence of content, and will turn away from a new thing if it is indifferently clothed. We often judge things quickly, by appearances, before knowing what they really are.

Sensibility precedes logic with us. Yet through the intermediary of the first we can be brought to examine the second. Literature brings precious help to science and wisdom, in order to assure the triumph of the truth and the virtue they preach.

In this respect, Islamic doctrine leaves nothing to be desired. It gives entire satisfaction by its outer form, for anyone listening to its language, as well as by its depths. The Qur'an, its vehicle, was and still remains the pinnacle of the Arabic word. The beauty of its style is universally admired. If one considers in abstract the literary qualities which it unites, one could even say that it represents the ideal of what a work of literature should be.

Let us say straight away that the beauty of Qur'anic language is sublime and majestic, not seductively entrancing; it seizes the heart rather than flattering the ear; gives rise to admiration not enchantment; amazes rather than excites; and arouses pleasure through repose not movement.

In the golden age of Arab eloquence, when language reached the apogee of purity and force, and titles of honour were bestowed with solemnity on poets and orators in annual festivals, the Qur'anic word swept away all enthusiasm for poetry or prose, and caused the Seven Golden Poems hung over the doors of the Kaʿba to be taken down. All ears lent themselves to this marvel of Arabic expression.

Its phonetic substance far removed both from the softness of the language spoken by the sedentary peoples and the crudity of the nomads, uniting in golden mean the gentleness of one and the firmness of the other, forming a harmonious sonority, a charm dreamed of by all.

The arrangement of its syllables more sustained than prose, yet less rigorous than poetry, giving enough variety during the course of a verse to sustain the interest of the listener, but maintaining sufficient homogeneity to prevent its general sense from being broken by pauses between chapters.[2]

Its vocabulary chosen from among the most common words, yet with no lapses into banality, and from among the most noble, while rarely committing the error of obscurity.

Endowed with an admirable economy of language, through which the smallest number of words are used to render the richest ideas, usually unexpressible without resorting to long, complicated sentences.

From this purity of expression, this extreme density of style, free of any superfluous term yet often very elliptic, one experiences such stunning clarity that the least instructed man of the people can say to himself, 'I have very well understood.' But at the same time there are such depths, such flexibility, such undertones, radiating from all its aspects like the multiple facets of a diamond, that all the sciences and arts of the Islamic world draw their eternal rules and principles from it.

It is often remarked upon that all men, distinguished or vulgar, superficial or insatiable searchers, rediscover themselves there. It is as if each formula matches each person according to his capacity. And all this on subjects which did not even figure among the themes of pre-Islamic literature, and which had rarely been touched upon by poet or orator except in the vaguest terms. Indeed, one can affirm without hesitation that, from the linguistic point of view, the Qur'an created a language as well as a style.

But that which seems truly superhuman to us is that the Qur'an is able to side-step what is a normal psychological law: logic and sensibility usually function in alternation and in inverse proportion, with the plenitude of one entailing the temporary eclipse of the other. With the Qur'an we witness constant cooperation between these two opposing states, across all subjects.

Beneath the continuous musicality which forms an even cloak over a diverse field of discourse, we can see words in their true meanings. Whether in a narrative context or as a line of reasoning, a legal or a moral ruling, the words act with a force that is at the same time didactic, persuasive and emotive. They appeal to heart and reason in almost equal proportions. What is more, while acting upon our various faculties, the discourse itself maintains, undisturbed throughout, its stunning gravity and powerful majesty.

We make haste to leave this subject now, for, without the verification with the text we have carried out elsewhere and cannot repeat here,[3] such an abstract enumeration of qualities has no real sense or value. Moreoever, a pure Arab, with the instinct for language in his blood, does not need analysis in order to appreciate the inimitable character of Qur'anic expression. He seizes by intuition what is here disengaged by the slow and discursive process of reasoning, and feels its celestial origin as it pierces his heart and dazzles his eyes.

The unbelievers of the time of the Prophet, immediately aware of this phenomenon, found themselves at a loss to explain it and called it magic. Even in our age, despite the passage of time, the inter-mingling of races and the adulteration of linguistic instincts, Arabs of all religions recognize the distinctive nobility which characterizes the Qur'anic text. This distinctiveness is not only in relation to the generality of Arabic literature, but also in relation to the words of the Prophet himself, themselves renowned for their eloquence.

We possess thousands of examples of the Prophet's own speech; some, like the *Ḥadīth al-Ifk*, the result of prolonged, month-long meditation, others instances of revelation that were not included in the body of the Qur'an. The revealed text is instantly recognizable, like a ray of sunlight against the light of candles. One immediately perceives a special tone, which does not seem to originate from man, and which could be nothing other than Divine breath.

Before leaving this chapter, we would like to elucidate on a point which has escaped not only the orientalists, but also certain eastern scholars: the manner in which the Qur'an deals with many different subjects in the same *sūra*.

Unable to see at first glance any overall unity or natural liaison between topics, some have regarded the Qur'an as nothing more than a chaotic and formless assemblage of disparate ideas, put together willy-nilly with no care for logic. Others have thought to attempt to justify this disparity as a device to relieve the boredom of uniformity and the mournful effect of monotony, both of which are repugnant to the Arab ideal of literature.

Some have tried to compensate for a lack of overall organization by identifying a poetic unity to each *sūra*, something it is impossible to render in translation. Yet others, indeed the majority of orientalists, have attempted to exonerate its author, saying that the Qur'an was given in isolated fragments out of sequence. They then attribute its incoherence to its compilers; it was they who brought together this unhappy mixture and reassembled the broken pieces by stringing them together into chapters.

But none of these explanations seems satisfactory to us. Tradition establishes the fact that the *sūra*s as we read them today received their titles and places during the lifetime of the Prophet, and there could only be an intrinsic defect, which the alleged explanations are unable to explain, if it were indeed the case that the unity of a *sūra* consisted of nothing but a sequence of letters and sounds clothing a fundamental dispersion, leaving ruptures of logic in the progression of ideas, and abrupt transitions from subject to subject.

If one wishes to appreciate the beauty of a design, one cannot look at just one small part taken out of context, where perhaps neighbouring colours may appear to jar. It is necessary to stand back, enlarge one's field of vision to take in the whole, in one all-embracing view. Only then will one be able to see the symmetry of parts and the harmony of composition hidden therein. This too, then, is how one should envisage the study of each chapter of the Qur'an if one is to judge it properly.

During our time at Al-Azhar, we tried to apply this rule to the study of one Medinan *sūra* (*al-Baqara*) and two Meccan *sūra*s (*Yūnus* and *Hūd*), not chosen for any reason other than their being prescribed on the syllabus. Well! We discovered more than we were looking for. We were looking to discover whether there was a logical sequence to the chain of ideas. To our astonishment, what emerged was a clearly delineated and organized plan, consisting of an introduction, a development and a conclusion.

Thus, in an small number of verses at the beginning of the *sūra*, the main lines of the subjects which it proposes to treat are indicated; the order of development then ensues in such a manner as to ensure not only that each part should not encroach on the next, but also that each parcel should find a definite place within the ensemble; finally comes the conclusion, corresponding exactly to the introduction.

If one considers the innumerable gaps between revelations and the extremely fragmentary manner in which the Qur'an was revealed, taking into account the fact that these revelations generally arose in answer to particular situations that had to be dealt with, one finds oneself wondering at what stage the task of putting the *sūra*s into their places was undertaken.

This question poses something of a dilemma, because whether one supposes that this was undertaken before, or after, the entire Qur'an had been revealed, one would assume that it would be arranged either chronologically, according to the sequence of appearance, or logically, according to the themes treated. The variegated aspect which the *sūra*s in fact offer us answer to neither rationale or organization, being neither simple nor natural.

This, however, brings us to conceive of a more complex plan, one which would have had to have been determined beforehand, even before the appearance of the text into the consciousness of the Prophet. Though we may initially feel dissuaded from such a hypothesis, thinking that it would be rather bold, if not absurd, to wish arbitrarily to establish a priori a predetermined order for discourses pronounced over a period of 20 years and connected with a thousand and one circumstances that could not have been foreseen or foreseeable, tradition supports us in this strange hypothesis.

Tradition tells us that, as and when it emerged, each fragment of the Qur'an, large or small, was allocated to one of the incomplete chapters, and to a determined place within that chapter, with each fragment numbered according to its place, in an order that was not always chronological. Once it had been given a place it was to remain there, never to be transferred nor reworked. There must therefore have been not only a plan for each *sūra*, but also an overall arrangement for the Qur'an, a plan according to which each new revelation was immediately slotted into place.

The manner of composition of the Qur'an, then, is absolutely unique. Never was a work, literary or otherwise, constructed in such a way. One could compare it to the process by which numbered pieces from an old, dismantled building are reconstructed in the same form as before in another place. How otherwise can we explain its immediate and systematic classification into various chapters, simultaneously brought to completion? The filled and unfilled pigeon-holes of this work must have constituted a single whole in the mind of the Author.

If a man wished to establish such a plan, what historical guarantee could he have of future events, their legislative requirements, the solutions necessary for them, the sentences in which they should be couched and their place in one chapter rather than another? And how could these sparse morsels, brought together with no retouching, soldering or evident joints, in spite of their natural variety and being scattered over a historical period – how could they form an organic body answering to the exigences of cohesion and beauty? Such an ambitious project could surely only proceed from a chimerical dream or a super-human Power.

In other words, if ruptures of logic or hiatuses in rhetoric would be the inevitable expected result if such a complicated and puzzling plan were devised by a human, does it not then follow that the success of such a plan presupposes the intervention of a transcendent Power with the capacity to establish such coordination? What creature could direct events so exactly that such an enterprise could succeed? Or how could such a work of art result from a series of chance events? Given such conditions, the logical unity and literary cohesion of Qur'anic *sūra* is, in our opinion, the miracle of miracles.

The principle of Qur'anic unity has already been proclaimed by innumerable competent authorities, among them Abū Bakr al-Naysābūrī, Fakhr al-Dīn al-Rāzī, Abū Bakr Ibn al-ʿArabī, Būrḥān al-Dīn al-Bikāʿī,[4] and Abū Isḥāq al-Shātibī. In order to verify it by means of a few samples, we could do no better than to refer to our study described above.

That these samples could serve as an exact model for the rest I cannot assert, for that would be to answer an empirical question with an a priori judgement. It is not inconceivable that in some chapters it would be more difficult to distinguish the principal idea, the way that related ideas are linked to each other and the kernel of the argument. Alternately, one might not know the particular circumstances which determined their association in thought. Furthermore, the density and richness of Qur'anic expression allows several points of reference to be established in each piece, with a multitude of possible linking threads. This means that different commentators will explain differently the links between the parts.

In one way or another, however, regardless of whether or not we know it precisely and whether or not the Prophet himself knew it precisely, there must have existed some sort of pre-determined plan.

Those who are not concerned with uncovering an organic plan in the text can readily admire another kind of plan, namely that of the stylistic order. Fragments destined to abut on each other are shaped to fit one next to the other, with no apparent discrepancy or fissure, regardless of the diversity of their subjects and the distance between the times of their appearance.

Our admiration reaches its peak, however, when we realize that these same fragments followed a very different lay-out when they first appeared. Let us follow through from beginning to end the gradual stages of the Qur'anic revelation during its 23 years.

From prophecy to preaching: *Read*,[5] to *Arise and warn*.[6]

From private initiation to solemn preaching:

> *Therefore declare openly what thou art commanded, and turn away from the polytheists.*
>
> 15:94

From a call addressed to close relatives, *And warn thy nearest relations,*[7] to one which would spread through the entire city, *And thy Lord never destroyed the towns, until He had raised in their metropolis a messenger, reciting to them Our messages,*[8] then to the surrounding towns, *that thou mayest warn the mother of the towns and those around her,*[9] and finally to all mankind, *We have not sent thee but as a mercy to the nations.*[10]

From the institution of basic foundations (the Meccan *sūras*) to their application (the Medinan *sūras*).

From the stigmatization of drink, *They ask thee about intoxicants and games of chance. Say: In both of them is a great sin and (some) advantage for men, and their sin is greater than their advantage,*[11] to its formal prohibition, *O you who believe, intoxicants and games of chance and (sacrificing) to stones set up and (dividing by) arrows are only an uncleanness, the devil's work; so shun it that you may succeed.*[12]

From endurance, *Hast thou not seen those to whom it was said: Withhold your hands, and keep up prayer and pay the poor-rate,*[13] to resistance, *And fight in the way of Allāh against those who fight against you but be not aggressors. Surely Allāh loves not the aggressors,*[14] and so on.

But from this entire process it is perhaps sufficient to retain two dates, the first and the last. The first is the Day of the Cave, when Muhammad was warned that he was to receive a Divine teaching:

> *Read in the name of thy Lord who creates – creates man from a clot. Read and thy Lord is most Generous, Who taught by the pen, taught man what he knew not.*
>
> 96:1-5

whose heavy weight he would have to bear:

> *Surely We shall charge thee with a weighty word.*
>
> 73:5

The last is the day of the farewell pilgrimage, when it was announced to him that his mission was completed and that he had nothing further to accomplish on earth:

> *This day have I perfected for you your religion and completed My favour upon you, and chosen Islām as your religion.*
>
> 5:3

After this there was no delay before he was recalled.

To conclude, then, everything developed according to a detailed plan of education and legislation conceived, from the very beginning and in its entirety, by the Inspirer. That these same texts, which in chronological order formed an impeccable pedagogical plan, should then immediately be taken out of their historical sequence, in order to be allocated and grouped into various defined frameworks of unequal size; and that from this predetermined dispersion a work should appear, destined to be read and composed of completely integrated sections, with each having a logical literary cohesion no less excellent than the overall line of argument: in this double arrangement we have a scheme which could not have proceeded from mere human knowledge.

Part Three
The Origin of the Qur'an

The study of the sources of a work would normally precede that of its contents, but in the case of the Qur'an we are forced to deviate from this rule. For not only does the concept of the Qur'an's Divine origin constitute part of its doctrine, it is at its very fundament.

From beginning to end, the Qur'an speaks to the Prophet, or speaks of him, but never does it allow him to express his own thoughts. It is God throughout Who expresses Himself, dictates, pronounces edicts, relates or warns. Time and again we find ourselves reading such phrases as o Prophet, o Messenger, We reveal to thee, We send thee, transmit this, recite that, do this, do not do that, they will say to thee, answer them and so on. Even where the text does not explicitly have a didactic approach towards the Prophet, for instance in the formula to be recited at prayer, the *Fātiha*, everything indicates that such an approach is intended.

But why can we not attribute Qur'anic language and its expressed ideas to the person who enunciates them; his own thoughts, or a reproduction of what he has picked up naturally from his ambience? How can we come to see this person as a simple receptacle, drawing his work from an exterior superhuman Entity? Such an assertion will unfailingly disconcert people, for it would appear to contradict the laws of psychology, at least in their ordinary manifestations. But Muhammad was definitely not the first to have posed the problem of revelation.

Yet Muhammad was even more modest in this respect than Moses. The latter, as the Qur'an confirms, received the Pentateuch through direct communication with the Eternal. For Muhammad, however, the Qur'an is the word of a celestial messenger, intermediate between God and himself:

> *Surely it is the word of a bountiful Messenger, the possessor of strength, established in the presence of the Lord of the Throne, one (to be) obeyed, and faithful.*
>
> 81:19-21

Nonetheless, despite this difference, each makes reference to the Supernatural.

Even for those who admit the principle of revelation in general, it is quite legitimate for them not to accept it in a specific case until all other possibilities for a natural explanation have been exhausted. To accept the immediate Divine origin of a phenomenon would be a final recourse; science's humble admission in default of finding any other cause.

Let us, then, give a brief outline of the argument which can be derived from the marvel that is Qur'anic style in favour of the Book's divinity. Simply ask yourself if the ideas which it contains can be explained by anything other than revelation.

Throughout the ages, there has been no lack of research into this subject. And one ought to mention, to the credit of the Qur'an and the *ḥadīth*, that there we can find, faithfully recorded and in great detail, all the hypotheses of this kind put forward by the Prophet's contemporaries. These hypotheses exhaust not only all the likely solutions, but also the absurd ones, which one will always find, invented by a spirit of mockery in order to hold a new enterprise up to ridicule, however serious that enterprise might be, and however crucial to humanity. Thus one could say that modern research can only develop or repeat in one form or another the strivings of bygone days.

The aim of the third section will be to chronologically examine these different explanations in their present form. We shall therefore divide them into two groups: those that refer to the time before the Hijra, and those that follow it.

7
Meccan Sources of the Qur'an

The most simplistic of the theories seek to uncover in the restricted area of the Hejaz, if not in the natal town of the Prophet itself, all the practical elements of Qur'anic doctrine. Ernest Renan supplies us with a typical example of this kind of approach in his article 'Mahomet et les Origines de l'Islamisme'.[1]

The French scholar offers us a picturesque view of Arabia in the sixth century. In place of the idolatrous people we all know, he describes for us a people who knew neither variety nor plurality in God, who had always conceived of Him as one who did not beget others and was not Himself begotten.[2]

Though Renan is right to underline the refined literary spirit and vivid sense of reality of this race, he leaves other, less honourable characteristics unmentioned. Hence, instead of an arrogant, debauched group of materialists, little concerned with speculation about the higher truth, he presents us with a society bubbling over with religious fervour. He has all religions and all civilizations meeting there, and tells us that everybody 'discussed religion'.[3] He would have us believe that Muhammad followed rather than perpetrated the religious trends of his time.

Yet the Qur'an itself provides us with a faithful picture of contemporary Arab life, and the scenario it paints for us is quite different. We have already seen the tissue of superstition with which the Arabs swathed their primitive monotheism. Their social and moral aspects, however, were no less deplorable. Thus we find infanticide:

> *They are the losers indeed who kill their children foolishly without knowledge ...*
>
> 6:141

prostitution:

> *... And compel not your slave-girls to prostitution when they desire to keep chaste ...*
>
> 24:33

and incest:

> *And marry not women whom your fathers married ... This surely is indecent and hateful; and it is an evil way. Forbidden to you are your mothers, and your daughters, and your sisters, and your paternal aunts, and your maternal aunts, and brother's daughters and sister's daughters ...*
>
> 4:22-3

Extortion of dowry:

> *And if you wish to have (one) wife in the place of another and you have given one of them a heap of gold, take nothing from it ... And how can you take it when one of you has already gone in to the other and they have taken from you a strong covenant?*
>
> 4:20-1

or a woman's inheritance:

> *O you who believe, it is not lawful for you to take women as heritage against (their) will. Nor should you straiten them by taking part of what you have given them, unless they are guilty of manifest indecency ...*
>
> 4:19

Similarly, we find evidence of the oppression of orphans:

> *... you should deal justly with orphans ...*
>
> 4:127

cupidity, negligence of the poor and contempt for the weak:

> *Nay, but you honour not the orphan, nor do you urge one another to feed the poor, and you devour heritage, devouring all. And you love wealth with exceeding love.*
>
> 89:17-20

Even the famous Arab virtue of *muruwwa* (hospitality, generosity) the Qur'an portrays for us as displaced charity, tarnished with the vices of prodigality and ostentation:

And those who spend their wealth to be seen of men and believe not in Allāh nor in the Last Day ...

4:38

In short, it was a life of *manifest error*,[4] of *ignorance*.[5] The pagan Arabs may have retained certain of the aspects of patriarchal religion in their practices, the rite of pilgrimage for example, but these were riddled with error and superstition:

They ask thee of the new moons. Say: They are times appointed for men, and (for) the pilgrimage. And it is not righteousness that you enter the houses by their backs, but he is righteous who keeps his duty ...

2:189

And when you have performed your devotions, laud Allāh as you lauded your fathers, rather a more hearty lauding ...

2:200

Amongst this mass of ignorant and misguided people there stood out a tiny elite. Known in the tradition by the name *ḥanīf*, they did not follow the multitude in their thinking. It is this small group which Renan took as representing the spirit of the age. Yet we know that they were in fact exceptions, who could be numbered on the fingers of both hands.

We have only to consult pre-Islamic literature to realize that most people remained impervious to such concerns. At the annual fair of ʿUkāẓ, for example, the assembly did not debate religion, but worldly glory. Each tribe showed off its poetic genius and invoked past and present knightly exploits. Likewise, in the celebrated Golden Odes 'hardly a single religious thought' is mentioned.[6]

And what was the actual doctrine of this elite of reformers, Muhammad's predecessors? Absolutely nothing, or as good as nothing. Their souls were dissatisfied with the polytheism and cruel, lax customs of their co-citizens, and they aspired to a healthy and holy religion which they tried to find outside this framework, but they had no precise conception of this religion. It could not be said to foretell, even from afar, the doctrine of the Qur'an. Zayd bin ʿAmr bin Nufayl, the most steady and independent amongst this group, solemnly avers that he does not know in what manner God should be adored.[7]

All that can be deduced from the example of the *ḥanīfs*, as Renan himself realized, is that there was 'a kind of uneasiness and vague sense of expectation' in this period, which manifested in these 'few privileged souls as presentiments and desires'.[8] These men used words such as 'God', 'cult', 'prophets', 'books' and 'paradise' without point; these words did not correspond in their spirit with any clear and distinct formulation.

If we wish, without leaving the birthplace of Islam, to speak of a religious system that may have been arrested in its growth, Sabaeanism, rather than Ḥanīfism, should be our focus. Did the term Sabaean in the Qur'an refer to a more refined sect of paganism (the Sabaeans of Ḥarrān claimed to belong to Ṣābī, son of Seth, to profess the latter's religion and to possess his book in Syriac) or to the Judaeo-Christian sect also known as the Mandeans, followers of John the Baptist? Or were they perhaps pagans disguising themselves under the ambiguous title of Christians?

The question is a controversial one. Al-Fayyūmī, for one, goes for the latter definition in his Arabic dictionary *al-Miṣbāḥ al-Munīr*. In any case, two considerations compel us to put aside the second hypothesis: firstly the discrepancy between the roots *ṣ-b-'* and *s-b-ḥ*, and secondly that the *ḥadīth* is conspicuously silent concerning the Sabaean doctrines of emanation and incarnation, although the fundamental and principal practices attributed to the Sabaeans are well identified and refuted in the Qur'an and *ḥadīth*.

Some of these ideas and practices had been adopted by the Qurayshites, and were so widespread that it is difficult to isolate them from the general current of paganism then abounding. Thus, for example, the divinity of angels and stars and their influence over terrestrial events;[9] the allocation of the lion's share of their sacrifices to the infernal powers, rather than to God;[10] the associatory formula of invocation which they used during their pilgrimage;[11] and so on.

However, certain other of their ritual or customary practices differ from both pagan and Muslim usage. For the Sabaeans, the pilgrimage was directed to the Iraqi town of Ḥarrān, and not to the Kaʿba; their sacrifices had to be burned in their entirety, not eaten;[12] they forbade bigamy; and they did not practise circumcision.[13] Even their prayers were obviously those of a cult directed to the heavenly bodies: enacted three times a day and coinciding exactly with the rising, the apogee and the setting of the sun, they were quite the opposite of the Islamic prescription.

Pure or gross, superstitious, sceptical or critical, the paganism of the Hejaz certainly cannot account for the origin of the Qur'an. Let us leave this area and look elsewhere. Perhaps the Judaeo-Christian milieux will bring some light to bear on the question.

We shall not expatiate upon the story of the Christian monk, Baḥīrā, who, tradition tells us, met Muhammad at the age of 12 during his journey into Syria with his uncle. Good sense precludes our taking this fleeting encounter as a source of instruction, for either we regard the account as legendary, or we take note of the facts related therein. That is to say the interview took place before the company of the whole caravan, Muhammad was the one who was interrogated, not the one who listened, and after his interrogation the monk concluded with a prophecy about the future mission of the young man. The idea that Muhammad learned anything from the monk is refuted by the account itself.[14]

Should we linger any longer to examine another hypothesis of a similar nature? We are told, for instance, that, lodging 'in the out-lying area' of Mecca,[15] were small-time adventurers, Romanies, Abyssinians, 'wine-sellers' and other 'riff-raff'. We are told that it was 'in the taverns that the Gospel was proclaimed to uncouth souls'.[16] So would it be there that Muhammad would have had contact with religious ideas? We are left with a vague statement, and given no documentation to support it.

We have several reasons, anyway, for not taking the possibility or fruitfulness of such contact seriously. In the first place, Muhammad's early movements are well known to us, and thoroughly demarcated by history. He was in solitude, shepherd of a flock; he was involved in full-scale trading ventures, as part of a caravan; and finally he played his part in noble society, amongst the leaders. Hence neither his customs, nor his birth, nor his successive occupations could lead one to imagine the Prophet in low dives.

In the second place, such contact would have been useless: not only did these frustrated souls knew their religion imperfectly,[17] but, as the Qur'an itself argues, their *foreign* tongue would create a natural barrier between them:

> *And indeed We know that they say: Only a mortal teaches him. The tongue of him whom they hint at is foreign, and that is clear Arabic language.*
>
> 16:103

And finally, if this were a possible source of information, would it not have been more natural and more within the scope of his adversaries to use this fact to scotch his ambition, instead of taking up arms at Medina, as we see happening later?

We prefer to speak of a much vaster and more cultivated milieu which could have contributed its ideas and religious practices to the formation of Islamic doctrine. We have seen that, during his youth, Muhammad had occasion to go to Syria on business from time to time and probably, too, to the Yemen: the journey of the winter and the summer. Now, we know that the Ghassanids of Syria and the Banī 'l-Ḥārith of Najrān in the Yemen had embraced Christianity, quite apart from the Jewish tribes of Medina and Khaybar which Muhammad would not have had contact with until later, after the Hijra.

As an intelligent observer, attentive by virtue of his vocation to moral matters, the Prophet would surely have been struck by the delicate customs and healthy ideas held by these societies, compared to those of his co-citizens, against whom he was so often indignant. Goldziher, among others, certainly believes so. The Hungarian author estimates that it was the contrast between the life and customs of his compatriots and the vivid impressions which he must have received in the course of his travels which gave him the first impulse towards reform.[18]

But will this explanation help us in resolving our problem? First of all, did Muhammad penetrate as far as the Christian territories proper? Certain writers doubt it very much, given the absence in the Qur'an of any mention of Christianity's exterior traits (though it does speak with more understanding of the profound spirit of oriental Christianity) in sharp contrast to the contemporary Arab poets who did visit these countries.[19] Other writers go even further, assuring us that the caravans undertaken by the Prophet did not take him beyond Sūq Hubāsha in the Tihāma, or Ghorash in the Yemen.[20]

Let us suppose ourselves in contact with the Christianity of those days and try to imagine whether he would have been enchanted by it. Let us consider some remarks from Christian authors. First of all, Sale:[21]

> If we read ecclesiastical history in detail, we see that, even from the third century, the Christian world was … disfigured by the ambitions of the clergy, by schisms, by controversies over the most absurd futilities, by endless disputes, divided and subdivided within themselves. The Christians … were so taken up with them, that it was as if they were vying with each other in malice, hate and mischievousness … They had in a certain sense chased Christianity from the world through their continual controversies on the question of how to interpret its doctrine. It was in these dark centuries that most of the superstitions and corruptions of the faith were not only perpetrated, but established … After the Council of Nicaea, the Oriental Church found itself torn apart by the disputes of the Arians, the Sabellians, the Nestorians and the Eutichians … The clergy … took it into their heads to give protection to army officers and under this pretext justice was sold publicly, and all types of corruption were encouraged. In the Western Church, the dispute between Damascene and Ursitan about the episcopal chair of Rome became so heated that they even resorted to violence and murder … That these dissensions arose was principally the fault of the emperors, in particular Constance … Though they were yet worse under Justinian … who believed that it was no crime to condemn a man to death for having different sentiments from his own. This corruption of custom and doctrine, amongst princes as much as amongst the clergy, was necessarily followed by a general depravity of the people. The sole goal of people from all conditions of life was to obtain money, by whatever means, and to dissipate it in luxury and debauchery.

Then Taylor, who writes in his *Ancient Christianity*:[22]

> What Muhammad and his caliphs met in every direction ... was superstition so abject, idolatry so gross and shameful, ecclesiastical doctrines so arrogant, religious practices so dissolute and puerile, that strong-spirited Arabs felt themselves freshly inspired, like the divine prophets, to condemn the errors of the world ...

Furthermore, one historian-monk, describing the sufferings inflicted by the Persians on the Palestinian people at the time of Muhammad, did not hesitate to blame on the wickedness of the Palestinian Christians God's sending the cruelty of the Zoroastrian persecutor against them. And, talking of the same period, Mosheim drew up a comparative picture between the latter-day and the first Christians and concluded that, during the seventh century, the true religion had been buried under a mass of senseless superstitions, and was incapable of raising its head.[23]

One could imagine that these works were written with a view to commenting on one extremely precise Qur'anic verse in *Sūrat al-Mā'ida*. This verse alludes to a certain distancing between Christianity and the then-contemporary Christians, and announces that the schism resulting from this alienation will last until the Day of Resurrection:

> *And with those who say, We are Christians, We made a covenant, but they neglected a portion of that whereof they were reminded so We stirred up enmity and hatred among them to the day of Resurrection. And Allāh will soon inform them of what they did.*
>
> 5:14

And did the converted Arab Christians behave themselves better than the original Christians? No. Indeed, in spite of their conversion, the Christian Arab tribes of pre-Islamic Syria did not desist from any of their pagan habits;[24] and ʿAlī could say of the Taghlib that the only thing they took from Christianity was the habit of drinking wine.[25] Huart concludes:[26]

> However seductive the idea might be that the practice of Christianity in Syria deeply affected the soul of the young reformer, it would have to be repudiated in the face of the uncertainty of any historical foundation to it.

Such, then, is the vivid spectacle which offered itself to our observer. Everywhere he went he met aberrations to be rectified, deviations to be brought back to the straight path. Nowhere did he see a firm moral and religious model on which he could have based his reform work. The materials he found will without doubt have given him something to demolish, hardly building blocks with which he could construct.

Let us now widen the field of our investigation beyond the concrete and visual world to the oral and literary milieu. If example had nothing to teach, maybe scholarly learning did, but whence could this learning have come, and through what medium?

The first possibility which comes to mind is that Muhammad could have derived his teachings from reading earlier revelations, Judaeo-Christian or otherwise.[27] But did Muhammad know how to read and write?

The Qur'an tells us not. Indeed, it describes his illiteracy as one of the proofs of the divinity of his source of instruction. For not only was the Prophet *ummī* (unlettered, uneducated), of an *ummī* people:

> *Those who follow the Messenger-Prophet, the Ummī ...*
>
> 7:157

> *Certainly Allāh conferred a favour on the believers when he raised among them a Messenger from among themselves ...*
>
> 3:163

> *He it is Who raised among the illiterates a Messenger from among themselves ...*
>
> 62:2

and not only did he, as Sprenger points out,[28] belong to a pagan people which had never before received any revelatory scriptures. The Qur'an affirms in clear-cut terms that Muhammad *didst not recite before it any book, nor didst thou transcribe one with thy right hand.*[29]

Muhammad's enemies themselves must certainly have recognized the Prophet's lack of education, for, wishing to explain the source of his knowledge of ancient history, they did not say that he must have written it, but that he must have had it written:

> *And they say: Stories of the ancients, which he has got written, so they are read out to him morning and evening.*
>
> 25:5

two very different forms which certain orientalists have confused with each other.[30]

Even supposing that the Prophet could read, there is yet another insurmountable obstacle: at that time there was no Bible in Arabic, neither an Old nor a New Testament.[31] Such foreign language documents were the monopoly of bilingual sages, who kept them preciously guarded. The Qur'an describes them as so avaricious of their knowledge that they would hardly concede to show a few sheets of the Pentateuch, taking great precautions in such instances to hide the rest of it:

> *... you make it into (scattered) papers, which you show and you conceal much ...*
>
> 6:92

At Medina, it denounced their other means of dissimulation:

> *And there is certainly a party of them who lie about the Book ...*
>
> 3:77

> *Woe! then to those who write the Book with their hands then say: This is from Allāh; so that they may take for it a small price ...*
>
> 2:79

In any case, history gives us no suggestion of any contact between the Prophet and the learned world before the Hijra. If one wishes to rely on uncontrolled generalities, one could doubtless assume the existence of such relations, opening the door to all kinds of speculation; but as soon as one has to be more precise, this all of a sudden seems blatantly anachronistic.[32]

So Muhammad could not have derived his religious ideas from Biblical texts, directly or through the methodical instruction of competent teachers. But is it not possible that he could have found them in the work of Arab poets, be they Judaeo-Christian or assimilated?

First of all, the Qur'an presents us with a Prophet so unfamiliar with poetry that he considers it a game not *meet for him*:

> *And We have not taught him poetry, nor is it meet for him ...*
>
> 36:69

But, had that not been the case, what kind of teaching could Muhammad have culled from this kind of literature?

Certain poets, al-Aʿshā for instance, depicted the customs and religious practices of the Church, notions of which no trace can be found in the Qur'an. They particularly concentrated on the imbibing of wine, which, far from borrowing, the Qur'an dealt a definite blow against. So the Qur'an cannot be linked with this kind of poetry.

Yet there is another genre of poetry which is almost entirely devoted to religious ideas. Our most striking example is the verses of Umayya bin Abī'l-Salṭ. His two favourite themes seem to be the description of future life and accounts of religious antiquity, often couched in the same terms as the

Qur'an. Why should we not see in them, then, the model on which the Qur'an was framed?

If we could establish the necessary conditions for making such an alignment, this would in fact be a most precious discovery, freeing us, once and for all, of the burden of giving supernatural explanations. We could say that the authors who saw the verses of Umayya as the link joining the Qur'an to the Bible surmised correctly.[33]

The first step necessary for us to uphold such a thesis would be the establishment, or postulation, of the authenticity of the verses in question. We do not intend to stir up difficulties on this point. Although our suspicions may be raised by literary collectors like Ḥammād and Khalaf al-Aḥmar, who fabricated verses and ascribed them to the ancients, mixing them in with their own, it would be excessively mistrustful to extend such behaviour into all Arab poetry in general, or all pre-Islamic poetry in particular.

Textual authenticity alone is not sufficient to establish one text as the original among two similar works: it must also be proven to be the anterior. This problem is historically insoluble in the context of the verses of Umayya and the Qur'an. Not only were Muhammad and Umayya contemporaries, and almost the same age, but Umayya continued to compose for about eight years after the last verse of the Meccan *sūra*s, in which certain resemblances with the verse of Umayya are to be encountered, had been revealed. It would, at the very least, be rather rash to maintain that his were the first in date.

Furthermore, Umayya never took it upon himself to be an original, nor did he pride himself on prophetic inspiration; he often admitted his deceit, and his regrets, in regard to this subject. This leads one to believe that he was drawn to make a pastiche, in a spirit of rivalry.

Muhammad, in contrast, always maintained in the most solemn manner that he did not gain his teaching from any man. Consider the enemies of the Prophet, always on the lookout for the slightest vulnerability they could use in their attacks on him, to turn him into a laughing stock. Would it not have been easier for them to point the finger at him for obviously plagiarizing such recent writing, than to direct their reasoning in all directions, trying all kinds of hypotheses and going as far as madness itself, in at attempt to explain the Qur'anic phenomenon?

Whence we conclude, if not with certainty, at least with a feeling of very great probability, that it was the Qur'an which served as the basis for the literature of its time, as it certainly was to do in the epoch which followed it.

And we do not wrong the poetic art if we state that, in contrast to the Qur'an, it does not guarantee the exclusivity of its sources. The poet is not so much concerned with the truth of the idea which he puts forward, as with the attractiveness of the form in which it is presented. He is free to seek his materials wherever he may find them: in the wisdom of the ancients or the moderns, in the facts of experience or in popular opinion, in sentiments or in absurd imaginings.

Now an internal critical faculty shows us in the verses of Umayya the presence of an entire range of different sources. Huart himself remarked upon it. Thus when the poet talks of hell, he borrows the language of the Bible; when he describes paradise, he uses Qur'anic terminology; when he speaks of sacred history, he has recourse to popular legend and to myth, where the same character is sometimes presented as a man, sometimes as an animal or a plant.

A final category remains in our exploration of possible exterior sources – popular culture.

We do not wish to go so far as to deprive the youthful Muhammad of any knowledge-by-hearsay of all preceding religions. It would seem to us untenable to pretend that he lived in splendid isolation, more ignorant than his own people, and these people do appear to us through the Qur'an as possessing some notion of previous revelations.

For example, they demand from the Prophet signs of divinity similar to those which his predecessors had brought:

> *... so let him bring to us a sign such as the former (prophets) were sent (with).*
>
> 21:5

contrast his doctrine of unity with what they understand of the last teaching that was revealed:

> *We never heard of this in the former faith: this is nothing but a forgery.*
>
> 38:7

and compare the cult of Jesus with that of their own idols:

> *And when the son of Mary is mentioned as an example, lo! thy people raise a clamour thereat. And they say: Are our gods better, or is he? They set it forth to thee only by way of disputation. Nay, they are a contentious people.*
>
> 43:57-8

It is easy to imagine that other elements of biblical knowledge were popularly disseminated, thanks to the mixture of religions that the Peninsula offered. However, several factors prevent us from giving too great a rein to our imagination: the lack of propaganda, and the dissimulation of the religious leaders; the rarity, the scattered nature, and above all the ignorance of those who converted; the racial prejudice of the ancient Arabs, and their lack of interest in questions that did not touch directly on their own immediate affairs or their own history; the absence in their literature, apart from one exception, of any religious themes.

It is very revealing to look at how much the attention of even those who had travelled and learned more was drawn to things unconnected with religious matters. Accordingly, al-Naḍr bin al-Ḥārith, when he wanted to try to compete with Qur'anic recitations, recounted to his audience the legends of the ancient kings of Persia and the exploits of its heroes, Rustam and Isfandiyar, not the history of patriarchs and prophets.[34] And what does the poet al-Nābigha al-Dhubyānī sing about in his poetry? King Solomon, Huart informs us.[35] It was always the glamour of worldly life that attracted them.

Faced with the effective silence of history on the degree of bookish knowledge this illiterate and indifferent people actually possessed, all that one can reasonably attribute to them are the rather vague and rudimentary notions discussed above. These could not throw much light on the origin of the Qur'an: neither its range, its precision, nor its profundity.

It is, in fact, inconceivable that these people of the time of *ignorance* could have shared to any degree the intellectual baggage of its few learned men. At no time in history, even with the most civilized and educated peoples, do we see such a rapprochement between the profane and the competent. Only he who possesses its secret can speak with exactitude and certainty about the atomic bomb; others can only eternally repeat its name, never knowing its formula. But this is a deductive piece of reasoning, valid only in the absence of any positive information.

The Qur'an itself does not remain silent on the novelty of its teaching to the Arabs, including the Prophet himself. Many times, in mentioning such and such episode of sacred history, it will state that Muhammad, no less than his own people, was not at all familiar with this history before he became acquainted with his mission:

> *This is of the tidings of things unseen which We reveal to thee. And thou wast not with them when they cast their pens (to decide) which of them should have Mary in his charge, and thou wast not with them when they contended one with another.*
>
> 3:43

> *These are announcements relating to the unseen which We reveal to thee; thou didst not know them – (neither) thou nor thy people – before this …*
>
> 11:49

> *We narrate to thee the best of narratives, in that We have revealed to thee this Qur'ān, though before this thou wast of those unaware.*
>
> 12:3

This is of the announcements relating to the unseen (which) We reveal to thee, and thou wast not with them when they resolved upon their affair, and they were devising plans.

12:102

If it were otherwise, what answer would he have heard from his adversaries?

Even supposing that certain details had infiltrated popular belief, could Muhammad so naively have given credence to the authority of the masses, when he had always shown himself as mistrustful of the learned?

And to which one current idea in that Babylon of religions would he have accorded the most credence; the pagans, the Sabaeans, the Magi, the Jews, and the Christians each presented truth in their own fashion. How would he have come to a firm conclusion amidst these contradictory statements? Indeed, if he had wished to tell us what each community, each sect, and each branch of each sect professed, what a monstrous mixture we should have had in the Qur'an:

And if it were from any other than Allāh, they would have found in it many a discrepancy.

4:82

Here it seems necessary to bring in a new factor: the personality coefficient.

One could suppose that during his brief retreats just before the first inspiration, or even during the pastoral solitude of his youth, this 'dreamer' might have dedicated himself to deep meditation on the real truth of such matters, and having reflected, made his choice.

A distinction must be made here between two domains of human knowledge: the empirical and the rational. Human history will not bend to our logic; there are absurdities in history which contradict our reasonings. Muhammad could not have discovered through turning in on himself that such and such an event happened at such and such a date. It is precisely the parallelism between sacred history in the Qur'an and the preceding scriptures that most often prompts the search for possible means by which such concordance could have been effected.

Since rational meditations have no effect on the empirical plane they are, without doubt, an excellent medium for the unveiling of eternal truths. What is the impact of pure reason on matters of religion? Very limited, one must admit. Of course, it does serve to expose falsity, stupidity, the folly of idolatry and superstition. But once these extravagances have been eliminated, what is to be built in their place? No doctrine has ever been founded on negative notions alone.

At this first stage, Muhammad must have found himself in the same position as the *ḥanīf*, that is to say, perplexed and anguished. At least, that is what the Qur'an leads us to believe. It describes him as heavy-hearted on the eve of the revelation, groaning as if weighed down by a crushing burden:

> *Have We not expanded for thee thy breast, and removed from thee thy burden, which weighed down thy back?*
>
> 94:1-3

We freely grant that the first stage of this research was covered fast, and the most fundamental truths soon, even early, uncovered. But to know God the Creator is not everything there is to religious knowledge in the Qur'an, and the path to this knowledge is very long and tortuous, if not completely closed to human intelligence.

By what illumination did Muhammad discover the incalculable Divine Attributes, the relationship between God and the visible and invisible worlds, the destiny which He reserved for man after death, without ever falling back on any previous truth but at the same time maintaining a striking concordance with the given facts of the scriptures as preserved by the learned?

It is clear that pure intelligence, unguided by positive teachings, is incapable of advancing with such a sure and clairvoyant step along this path. And the Qur'an confirms this truth with relation to our current case, declaring that when Muhammad was taken over by the revelation, he knew nothing of faith or scripture, quite apart from the diverse aspects of legislation contained in the Qur'an, be they moral, social or ritual.

In what ways should a cult to God be established? What is the best code of conduct for the individual, for society and for humanity? Of all this Muhammad was ignorant. Would he have known how to guide others in religious matters when he did not know how to guide himself?:

> *And find thee groping, so He showed the way?*
>
> 93:7

8

Medinan Sources of the Qur'an

Whether a change of milieu and contact with peoples possessing scriptures had any effect on the conduct of the Prophet or his teaching

After the rapid tour of the horizon we have just completed, which ended everywhere in a negative result, we might be tempted to immediately go on to our conclusions, were it not for the fact that there was a change in the course of the Prophet's mission.

This change does not come about at the beginning of the revelatory period, and that is why we have dealt with the Meccan phase as a whole, making no distinction between the time before and during revelation. Though, since it is a matter of trying to find a human origin for the Qur'an we ought to have, and still should, set aside the possibility that the Qur'an is a self-originated phenomenon.

But putting this argument to one side for the time being, we can state that during the first half of Muhammad's mission, that is to say during his sojourn in Mecca, not only did the conditions of his surroundings remain unchanged, but the possibility of his having access to exterior information tended to diminish.

As soon as the Prophet launched his first message, he emerged into history proper. More and more were his steps counted, his relations with others observed, and, while the opposition and the persecution steadily increased, so did his independence, his conviction and the tone of authority in his teaching.

Given the extreme dearth, if not the total lack, of usable sources during the pre-Hijra period, the hypothesis that Muhammad may have received instruction from a human source now tends to be pretty much abandoned after the Hijra.

With the Hijra, however, a considerable change did take place: Muhammad was transported from a pagan, ignorant and hostile environment to a welcoming, friendly atmosphere, surrounded by strong and devoted disciples. Furthermore, from this point on he was in contact with an organized religious community in possession of a sacred Book, namely the Jews of Medina. Would there not be in this new era and this new environment fruitful ground for historical research and doctrinal rapprochement?

Let us consider first of all the general disposition of the Qur'anic spirit, even well before the Hijra, to see whether it would have truly seen this new environment as representing revealed virtue and, in consequence, worthy of emulation.

It is strange to observe the striking contrast between the Qur'anic attitude towards the Judaic world, and its attitude towards Christians. When it speaks specifically about Christians, if it does not exactly praise them:

> *... and thou wilt find the nearest in friendship to the believers to be those who say, We are Christians ...*
>
> 5:82

it at least accords blame in a relatively attenuated tone:

> *And with those who say, We are Christians, We made a covenant, but they neglected a portion of that whereof they were reminded so We stirred up enmity and hatred among them to the day of Resurrection ...*
>
> 5:14

It is not the same when it turns to the Jews of the time, or the People of the Book in general. To the Qur'an, these are no longer people who follow the revelation, but rather they are satanically inspired:

> *By Allāh! We certainly sent (messengers) to nations before thee, but the devil made their deeds fair-seeming to them. So he is their patron to-day ...*
>
> 16:63

Alluding to the torture by fire in the ditch, which the Jews of the Yemen had inflicted upon Christians, it takes the side of the latter, pronouncing this crime a premeditated attack against true belief:

Destruction overtake the companions of the trench! – the fire fed with fuel – when they sit by it. And they are witnesses of what they do with the believers. And they punished them for naught but that they believed in Allāh
85:4-8

Later, in Medina, not only does the Qur'an maintain this position; it increases its condemnation. Those who have received the Pentateuch and cultivated the letter of the law, it proclaims, do not observe it with faith:

The likeness of those who were charged with the Torah, then they observed it not, is as the likeness of the ass carrying books …
62:5

They practice usury and take advantage of all kinds of illicit means of gaining wealth:

And for their taking usury – though indeed they were forbidden it – and their devouring the property of people falsely …
4:161

Thanks to a religious illusion, they allow themselves to corrupt and lie:

Woe! then to those who write the Book with their hands then say, This is from Allāh; so that they may take for it a small price … And they say: Fire will not touch us but for a few days …
2:79-80

They believe that they cannot be held to any kind of justice, nor do they have any obligation towards other communities:

… and among them is he who, if thou entrust him with a dīnār would not pay it back to thee, unless thou kept on demanding it. This is because they say there is no blame on us in the matter of the unlearned people …
3:75

Is it not astonishing to suppose that these people whom the Qur'an judges so severely could serve as a model, or a source of instruction? Nonetheless, however illogical this hypothesis may be, it ought not prevent us from examining its argument.

An a priori judgement can be contradicted by facts, and one must welcome with gratitude all serious research that has for its aim the disclosure of an unknown corner of the truth. Doubt as method (Descartes) is, in our eyes, a salutary principle, as indispensible to faith as it is to knowledge.

After all, what is the good of having a faith built upon moving sand? Error and its favourite stronghold, the prejudiced, are every sincere conscience's biggest enemy: it must always be sought out and chased away, even if it is concealed behind truths which would seem to be sufficiently demonstrated.

When we see the moon changing phases according to its position in relation to the sun, we judge correctly that it is from the sun that it gains its light. Should we judge the Muhammadan revelations in the same way, when we see them evolve, modify themselves or retract in relation to their contact with the intellectual environment of Medina? That is what several European authors have tried to establish.

Without searching too deeply, most of them have been struck by two general aspects that they have regarded as incompatible with the divinity of the message. Their greatest argument centres around the belligerent attitude that was adopted in Medina, which seemed to be an about-turn in comparison with the previous period. When one adds to this the polygamy of the Prophet near the end of his life, Islamic morality in its final phase is totally ruined in their eyes; though they may well recognize the highest value in the suffering, persecuted, emergent Islam at Mecca and its pacifist, monogamous founder, they are unable to look without horror at 'his hands steeped in blood, surrounded by his cortège of women'.

The basis of argumentation easily discernible beneath the impressionistic style of these Christian authors cannot be taken seriously, for if they argued otherwise it would destroy part of their own faith in the final biblical teaching of Christ. This double argument must needs be invoked in its defence. Does it not, then, proceed from sentiment rather than from rigorous reasoning?

We have already sufficiently demonstrated the real position of Qur'anic law regarding the first argument above.[1] There is therefore no need to repeat it here.

As for the second argument, it hardly touches upon the object of our study, which is the Qur'an, and not the person of the Prophet. But, seeing as the Book does shed some light on the private life of its Messenger, we shall demonstrate what it shows.

From the Qur'an we can reconstruct an intimate portrait of the Prophet through the following qualities: sensibility, will and faith.

By his very nature he was, of course, a human being like his predecessors:

> *And We sent not before thee any but men to whom We sent revelation; so ask the followers of the Reminder if you know not. Nor did We give them bodies not eating food, nor did they abide.*
>
> 21:7-8

Like everyone else, he had to feed himself and try to earn a living:

> *And We did not send before thee any messengers but they surely ate food and went about in the markets ...*
>
> 25:20

He had wives and children, like several of the others:

> *And certainly We sent messengers before thee and appointed for them wives and children ...*
>
> 13:38

and he was not above the simple appreciation of human beauty:

> *It is not allowed to thee to take wives after this, nor to change them for other wives, though their beauty be pleasing to thee ...*
>
> 33:52

But since we are agreed on defining morality here – control over his own desires rather than insensibility – we must bring in a second factor: will. In this respect we see Muhammad capable of such strong abstention that he absolutely forbids himself things that are permitted, simply in order to avoid misunderstanding:

> *O Prophet, why dost thou forbid (thyself) that which Allāh has made lawful for thee?*
>
> 66:1

Thus it was that ʿĀ'isha said that no one had such mastery over his senses as he had.[2]

Finally, the Prophet submitted himself absolutely to the Divine commandments. This transcended his personal views and tendencies. Let us cite, in order of occurrence, the Qur'anic rules which first of all laid down the categories of women whom he could marry:

> *O Prophet, We have made lawful to thee thy wives whom thou hast given their dowries, and those whom thy right hand possesses, out of those whom Allāh has given thee as prisoners of war, and the daughters of thy paternal uncles and the daughters of thy paternal aunts, and the daughters of thy maternal uncles and the daughters of thy maternal aunts who fled with thee; and a believing woman, if she gives herself to the Prophet, if the Prophet desire to marry her ...*
>
> 33:50

and then, at a given moment, formally forbade him to undertake a new marriage, however much he wished to, or to substitute other wives for the ones he had.

These regulations culminated in the case of the divorced wife of the Prophet's adopted son Zayd, the only marriage specifically mentioned in the Qur'an:

> *And when thou saidst to him to whom Allāh had shown favour and to whom thou hadst shown a favour: Keep thy wife to thyself and keep thy duty to Allāh; and thou concealest in thy heart what Allāh would bring to light, and thou fearedst men, and Allāh has a greater right that thou shouldst fear Him. So when Zaid dissolved her marriage-tie, We gave her to thee as a wife, so that there should be no difficulty for the believers about the wives of their adopted sons, when they have dissolved their marriage-tie. And Allāh's command is ever performed.*
>
> 33:37

We see Muhammad trying to avoid this union, but having it imposed upon him by Qur'anic law in order to put an end (not only by teaching, as the Prophet had wanted, but also by example) to the pagan regime of adoption, by virtue of which the adopted son was made an entirely legitimate son. We could literally call this a duty marriage, contracted despite the strongest of feelings against it.

When we examine the circumstances under which the Prophet's other marriage contracts took place, we find that most were imposed, certainly not by such necessary legislation, but by other, more human considerations. To console and honour the widow of a martyr, for instance, or of someone who died while emigrating with his companions; in several instances to cement a co-tribal union by the bond of sacred parenthood; to create a favourable atmosphere when captives of an entire tribe were freed, after having already been in the hands of the Muslims, in the light of their new relationship with the Prophet; and so on.

But one does not have to be an erudite historian in order to be able to appreciate the moral character of a man who passed his youth in absolute chastity then, once married, observed the most loyal monogamous state for 30 years, and who finally took a second wife at the age of 55.[3] If one considers, moreover, Muhammad's occupations and preoccupations, his responsibilities and his very varied concerns, both public and private, his leading the five prayers from dawn to night, teaching the Qur'an, distributing the communal alms, resolving disputes, receiving delegations, corresponding with kings and governors, commanding expeditions, constituting the law, founding an empire – basically, to concern himself with everything – and on top of that his keeping vigil at night, prostrate, on his knees, or standing, regarding the heavens, one is led to think that motives other than self-gratification must have been behind the institution of polygamy.[4]

Certain orientalists have taken their research into the sacred text of Islam further than these popular objections against war and polygamy. They believe they have found a radical difference between the two periods in the Qur'anic teaching.

In Mecca, the Judaeo-Christian stories in the Qur'an remained 'in a sketchy state'.[5] It was at Medina that the first encounters with the Jews enabled Muhammad 'to familiarize himself with the history of Abraham and the genealogical relationships with Ismāʿīl and the Arab people'.[6] He had 'lived first of all under the agreeable illusion that his preaching, his Qur'an, corresponded completely with the holy Books of the Jews and Christians. The sharp opposition of the Jews of Medina convinced him to the contrary.'[7]

Similarly, in the beginning the prayer took place twice a day, morning and evening. At Medina a third was added, that of the afternoon, 'evidently in order to imitate the customs of the Jewish community.'[8] The day of 'Āshūrā' was instituted for the same reason, as was the orientation of the prayer towards Jerusalem,[9] both concessions which were later to be retracted because of the hostility of the Israelites.[10] Thus, ritual reflected political change.[11] Even the concept of God was modified under the influence of the bellicose attitude of the Medinan period: 'His sternness against hardened mischief-makers was combined with His quality of mercy.'[12]

Let us go back to the beginning and see whether there is any substance to these observations.

As regards the Judaeo-Christian stories in general, we are afraid to say that we have found nothing which could justify, either remotely or directly, such a remark. A simple consultation of the text reveals quite the contrary: it is in the Meccan *sūra*s that we find laid out in their smallest detail the diverse episodes of Biblical history.[13] All that was left to the Medinan period was the task of drawing lessons from these, often from the briefest of allusions.

As regards the particular question of Abraham, I do not know of another people with such a pronounced taste for the science of genealogy as the Arabs. Their members tenaciously kept the succession of their ancestors alive in their memories, often as far back as 20 generations. Is it likely that such a people lived in ignorance of their origin until the last moment? If the existence in their midst of the temple of the Kaʿba, parts of which carried the names of Abraham and Ismāʿīl, did not constitute for them a living and permanent witness of their link with these glorious names, they must have known through the Jews who were their neighbours for several centuries before the Hijra.

In any case, the Qur'an does not appear to have awaited Muhammad's transfer to Medina in order to establish this link – the Meccan *sūra*s already mention it:

> [Abraham said] *Our Lord, I have settled a part of my offspring in a valley unproductive of fruit near Thy Sacred House, our Lord, that they may keep up prayer …*
>
> 14:37

More than that, they enjoin the Prophet to follow the Ḥanīfite confession of Abraham:

> *Then We revealed to thee: Follow the faith of Abraham, the upright one; and he was not of the polytheists.*
>
> 16:123

And did the attitude of Islam with regard to the preceding religions evolve in its new residence? Here again we have recourse to the text.

In the Meccan *sūra*s, the Qur'an constantly calls to witness the people who have knowledge of the Scriptures:

> *… Say: Allāh is sufficient for a witness between me and you and whoever has knowledge of the Book.*
>
> 13:43

We see it make a stand against those possessors of Scripture who have followed Satan and allied themselves with him:

> *By Allāh! We certainly sent (messengers) to nations before thee, but the devil made their deeds fair-seeming to them. So he is their patron to-day …*
>
> 16:63

At Medina he maintains his position with regard to the scholars whose knowledge he always takes as witness, though a certain number amongst them do not wish to bear this witness:

> *… And those who have been given the Book certainly know that it is the truth from their Lord …*
>
> 2:144

> *Those whom We have given the Book recognize him as they recognize their sons. And a party of them surely conceal the truth while they know.*
>
> 2:146

In both of these cases, the Qur'an makes a clear distinction between the holy Books and the scholars who follow them faithfully on the one hand, and, on the other, those who call themselves Jews or Christians but follow nothing other than their own desires.

As far as the number of Muslim prayers is concerned, we must say that in all the Muslim works which we have been able to consult, we have nowhere found any indication of such an evolution. It is regrettable that the Western critics do not tell us from which sources they have derived this idea. According to all the information at our command, Muslim prayers numbered five from the very first hour of their institution at Mecca. The Prophet established them thus with all the necessary precision, and the Qur'an makes brief reference to them in several places:

> *So glory be to Allāh when you enter the evening and when you enter the morning. And to Him be praise in the heavens and the earth, and in the afternoon, and when the sun declines.*
>
> 30:17-18

> *... celebrate the praise of thy Lord before the rising of the sun and before its setting, and glorify (Him) during the hours of the night and parts of the day, that thou mayest be well pleased.*
>
> 20:130

> *And keep up prayer at the two ends of the day and in the first hours of the night ...*
>
> 11:114

> *Keep up prayer from the declining of the sun till the darkness of the night, and the recital of the Qur'ān at dawn ...*
>
> 17:78

Perhaps a misunderstanding slipped into the minds of these authors through an inadequate interpretation of the word *dulūk* in the last of these passages?

As for the day of ʿĀshūrā', to which the Qur'an does not allude, we know from the traditionists that the Qurayshites practised the fast on this day before the advent of Islam, and that the Prophet himself observed it before the Hijra.[14] We know, furthermore, that this observance remains recommended by the *ḥadīth*.[15] To say that the Prophet took his original decision in order to imitate the Jews, and then reversed this decision because of political changes, would be to make statements that do not fit the facts.

And as for the *qibla*, while it is true that the believers briefly, at the beginning of the Hijra, turned to Jerusalem to perform their prayer, it would be anachronistic to suggest that the hostility of the Jews somehow caused this direction to be replaced by that of the Kaʿba. Hostilities did not commence until 625, while the definitive regulation of the *qibla* took place in 623. Moreover this replacement is sufficiently explained in the Qur'an:

> *The fools among the people will say: "What has turned them from their qiblah which they had?" Say: The East and the West belong only to Allāh; He guides whom He pleases to the right path ... We shall surely make thee master of the qiblah which thou likest; turn then thy face towards the Sacred Mosque ...*
>
> 2:142-4

All that now remains is the Qur'anic concept of God. Reference to the text will show us whether the God of Islam changed, as far as the Qur'an's representation of Him is concerned, between the pre- and post-Hijra periods.

The Qur'an always speaks of God as universal Retributor for the good as much as for the bad, and the Meccan *sūra*s accordingly furnish us with both modes of retribution:

> *... Surely thy Lord is Quick in requiting (evil), and He is surely the Forgiving, the Merciful.*
>
> 6:166

> *... And surely thy Lord is full of forgiveness for mankind notwithstanding their iniquity. And surely thy Lord is Severe in requiting.*
>
> 13:6

The *sūra*s revealed at Medina, just as much as those at Mecca, begin with *In the name of Allāh, the Beneficent, the Merciful*. It is hence patently unnecessary for us to set out to prove that the love of God for those who were charitable, just, patient and pure, and His hatred for the unjust, the proud and the unfaithful, are presented without change in the two periods.

What does deserve to be contradicted is the specific remark put forward by our critics, for it is, in fact, in the Meccan *sūra*s that the God of battle appears the most frequently. It is here that we find the histories of a transgressing antiquity, and the terrible punishments undergone as a consequence: they act as a constant, implicit warning to towns in the process of taking the same path.

Furthermore, if we examine the text more closely, we can see that the struggle ordained against the aggressors at Medina was no less than the execution of an explicit ultimatum already given at Mecca:

What do they wait for, then, but the like of the days of those who passed away before them? ...

10:102

And say to those who believe not: Act according to your power, surely we too are acting; and wait, surely we are waiting (also).

11:121-2

And there is not a town but We will destroy it before the day of Resurrection or chastise it with a severe chastisement. That is written in the Book.

17:58

Underlying this last objection, as at the origin of so many others, is an error we would like to talk more about: the idea which is often formed of the notion of *naskh* (abrogation) in Islam.[16] This notion was sometimes seen by the Islamicists as the retraction of an order, sometimes as the discovery of a truth previously unknown. Yet neither the one nor the other definition correspond exactly to what is really intended.

In the realm of knowledge, there is never, nor could there ever be, an abrogator or an abrogated in revealed doctrine: yesterday's truth could not be yesterday's mistake. For then 'abrogation' would mean 'knowledge recently acquired', which would be an impiety if applied to God, not to say an absurdity.

But in the practical domain there have been abrogations, as much at the heart of one faith as from one faith to another – You have been told such; I say to you such and such other. In what sense should we understand such a change? For a law to be abrogated, must it have been inimical or badly conceived in the first place?

Though such thinking is admissible in our human institutions, it certainly is not when it is a matter of Divine law. God never goes back on His decisions, and He does not change His mind. Both the rule whose application He causes to cease and that which He substitutes for it carry the stamp of sanctity. Each of them is the imposition of wisdom for the time for which they were made. Whether it is a matter of progress or regression, of indulgence or severity, it is not in the concept of Legislator that the change resides; but in changing historical circumstances and the subsequent need for varied solutions.

Sometimes, the text which establishes the first measure expressly carries the title of 'provisional law':

... But pardon and forgive, till Allāh bring about His command.

2:109

> ... *call to witness against them four (witnesses) from among you; so if they bear witness, confine them to the houses until death takes them away or Allāh opens a way for them* [through new legislation].
>
> 4:15

but, more often than not, this classification is implied. One does not realize it until the other law has followed. This could give the impression of an improvised solution, but in reality everything was planned in advance and exactly scaled to fit determined eventualities:

> ... *And We did not make that which thou wouldst have to be the qiblah but that We might distinguish him who follows the Messenger from him who turns back upon his heels* ...
>
> 2:143

We would all agree that a good legislator would not treat men in their transitional phase in the same manner that he would when their evolution was complete. On the contrary, just like a doctor, he would change their regimen according to the development of their aptitude and capacity for assimilation. Far from being a fault, this progression in doctrine and legislation is the most appropriate method for forming clear, mature souls, disciplined nations and solid customs.

The observations by European authors we have just examined have as their central objective the need to prove, by internal analysis of Qur'anic teachings, the existence of borrowings from religious documents in Medina. The only way they could have succeeded in this aim would have been indirectly, establishing a connection between the information the Prophet had, and that possessed by people of the Scriptures.

But why should we not take the direct route, and put our finger on the person or persons from whom Muhammad could have sought instruction? No historian aware of his responsibility to objective knowledge has dared to do it, but how could it be that, living amongst them, this man could have had no contact with Jewish savants? What was their attitude towards him?

The Qur'an tells us, and divides them into classes.

The majority, already hostile long before Muhammad's arrival in their territory, not only hid their knowledge from him, but on many occasions tried fruitlessly to deceive him and lay traps for him. Sometimes, through the mediation of their co-citizens, they asked him awkward questions about revelation:

> *And they ask thee about the revelation. Say: The revelation is by the commandment of my Lord* ...
>
> 17:85

or historical mysteries like the Seven Sleepers.[17] At other times they demanded of him that he cause a book written in heaven to descend upon them; and they denied certain articles of faith which figured in their scriptures, but they did not keep unless they were challenged and shown up for their fraud:

All food was lawful to the Children of Israel, before the Torah was revealed, except that which Israel forbade itself. Say: Bring the Torah and read it, if you are truthful. So whoever forges a lie against Allāh after this, these are the wrong-doers.

3:92-3

And how do they make thee a judge and they have the Torah wherein is Allāh's judgement? ...

5:43

Hence we see a far from benevolent attitude on the part of people one might have thought able to initiate the Prophet.

But a certain number of Israelite scholars did come, free of racial prejudice and irrespective of personal ambition, to listen to the teaching of the Prophet and examine his face. Recognizing it immediately by certain precise signs contained in their Books, they bore witness to him of the divinity of his mission:

Those to whom We have given the Book follow it as it ought to be followed. These believe in it ...

2:121

Those whom We have given the Book recognize him as they recognize their sons ...

2:146

Those who follow the Messenger-Prophet, the Ummī, whom they find mentioned in the Torah and the Gospel. He enjoins them good and forbids them evil ...

7:157

And when Jesus, son of Mary, said: O Children of Israel, surely I am the messenger of Allāh to you, verifying that which is before me of the Torah and giving the good news of a Messenger who will come after me, his name being Aḥmad. But when he came to them with clear arguments, they said: This is clear enchantment.

61:6

The most famous name in this group is ʿAbd Allāh bin Sallām, and the circumstances in which he testified very edifying. This man, who had been recognized by the Jews as the most learned and virtuous amongst them up until that point, was immediately disowned by them upon the declaration of his conversion.[18]

Between these two categories of hostility and submission, history leaves no place for 'friendly teachers'. To say that Muhammad might have got his instruction from ʿAbd Allāh bin Sallām would not only require altering the story as given, reversing the roles of master and disciple; it would at the same time be an evident anachronism.[19] All the substance of scriptural truth was given and specified at Mecca, before these people even had the opportunity to 'see the face of the Prophet'.[20] And a large part of the several complementary episodes invoked at Medina are connected with Christian truth, which the Jews do not recognize.

From this point onwards, resemblances between Qur'anic exposition and Judaeo-Christian teachings are accumulated in vain,[21] not so much useless, as literally fabricating arms given by the Qur'anic thesis itself:

> *And surely the same is in the Scriptures of the ancients. Is it not a sign to them that the learned men of the Children of Israel know it?*
>
> 26:196-7

> *Surely this is in the earlier scriptures, the scriptures of Abraham and Moses.*
>
> 87:18-19

But there still remains a vast difference between self-admitted concordance and borrowings.

Conclusion

We have examined in the light of the facts the hypothesis of a human origin for Qur'anic doctrine. We have pursued its founder the length of his double career, secular and sacred. We have looked at the town of his birth and his final residence; his journeys and his relationships; his capacity to read and the availability of documents.

All the means of investigation that we possess are unable to convince us with any authority of the existence of straightforward physical means through which Muhammad could have had such contact with holy doctrines. Even if we persuade ourselves to exaggerate his personal knowledge through hearsay, or augment the effects of the influence of his environment, these are not sufficient explanation for the extremely extended and precise detail of the colossal religious, historical, moral, legislative and cosmological work which is the Qur'an.

On the contrary, along with the prodigious phenomenon of inspiration, the Qur'an shows us the veritable whirlpool that took place in Muhammad's life, turning him from man to Prophet. Here we have two lives clearly separated:

> *Say: If Allāh had desired, I would not have recited it to you, nor would He have made it known to you. I have lived among you a lifetime before it ...*
>
> 10:16

Everything we know of Muhammad's secular career is reduced to one essential truth:

> *And surely thou hast sublime morals.*
>
> 68:4

During his youth, his biographers tell us, he was known by the name Trustworthy, a man faithful and honest. In his daily occupations he never allowed himself a dishonest act, nor did he participate in an idolatrous cult. Even his enemies avow that he never lied: the most solemn testimony we possess was made by the chief of the opposing faction, Abū Sufyān, who was only to embrace Islam two years later. The Roman emperor Heraclius concluded of him, If he does not lie to men, he is incapable of lying about God.[1]

But apart from these, and other similar, practical characteristics, no light is shed on any prior doctrinal knowledge, nor on a sense of prophetic vocation. Muhammad did not know what a scripture was, nor the meaning of faith. He was as unfamiliar with sacred history as his people:

> *This is of the tidings of things unseen which We reveal to thee. And thou wast not with them when they cast their pens (to decide) which of them should have Mary in his charge, and thou wast not with them when they contended one with another.*
>
> 3:43

> *These are announcements relating to the unseen which We reveal to thee; thou didst not know them – neither thou nor thy people – before this ...*
>
> 11:49

> *And thou wast not at the side of the mountain when We revealed to Moses the commandment ...*
>
> 28:44

He did not expect to play the part of one inspired by God:

> *And thou didst not expect that the Book would be inspired to thee, but it is a mercy from thy Lord ...*
>
> 28:86

He did not even know how to guide himself:

> *And find thee groping, so He showed the way?*
>
> 93:7

Could the Prophet have tried to enquire into the laws of nature, or asked himself questions about them? Maybe, but his answers could not have transcended the vague notions one might call natural religion. True knowledge and precise information in every domain would only be received by him, drop by measured drop, over a space of 23 years.

Everyone knows that the Qur'an appeared in a way that was fragmentary, intermittent and instantaneous. We can attach a more or less precise date to each transmission, and Muhammad's contemporaries were very often present, first of all as eye-witnesses to the exterior signs of the mysterious phenomenon of inspiration, and then as listeners of the admirable Text which issued forthwith.

It was for Muhammad a lived experience, never provoked: something he allowed to take place in complete passivity. He could neither escape from it nor prepare himself to receive it when he had need.[2]

It is here that one should seek the true source of his instruction. Each lesson was for him a new and unedited chapter for his store of knowledge, a lantern whose rays were extinguished just where the vibrations of the text stopped. Beyond this light, the Prophet had ordinary human capacities. He modestly and loyally put a great big question mark before the past, the future, everything that was impenetrable to the light of healthy human intelligence.

Whence did this inspiration gush forth? Was it not from the depths of his own soul?

Facts prove the contrary. First of all, the ideas transmitted by these inspirations generally took on an empirical or supra-rational character; thus they were excluded from the domain of pure intellect, as they were from sentiment limited to its ordinary resources. But what is more remarkable, and makes a striking contrast with the inspirations of poets and philosophers, is that it was not a question of ideas welling forth, it was pure phonetic audition. Not only did the ideas not precede the words; they were not even concomitant.

For the Prophet himself, this auditive phenomenon was initially somewhat disconcerting. Wishing to capture an elusive discourse which he was to transmit in its entirety to his people, he felt himself obliged to repeat it to himself, word for word, as it was being received. Indeed, he did not cease to use this procedure until he was given a formal instruction to desist, and a guarantee that God would teach and explain it to him:

> *Move not thy tongue therewith to make haste with it. Surely on Us rests the collecting of it and the reciting of it. So when We recite it, follow its recitation. Again on Us rests the explaining of it.*
>
> 75:16-19

On Us rests the explaining is a phrase which needs underlining, because it means that we are dealing here with textual inspiration, pure and simple.

Moreover, it is well known what an infinitely pious attitude the Prophet always maintained towards the revealed Text, and with what conviction he held it to be the word of God. It is inconceivable that he might have made the slightest change in it:

> *… Say: It is not for me to change it of my own accord …*
>
> 10:15

If he wished to interpret it, he did so in the manner of a commentator on a text not his own. Compare:

> *Ask forgiveness for them or ask not forgiveness for them. Even if thou ask forgiveness for them seventy times, Allāh will not forgive them …*
>
> 9:80

with:

> *It is alike to them whether thou ask forgiveness for them or ask not forgiveness for them – Allāh will never forgive them …*
>
> 63:6

We see him tremble at the idea of attributing to God anything, however slight, that He has not said:

> *And if he had fabricated against Us certain sayings, We would certainly have seized him by the right hand, then cut off his heart's vein. And not one of you could have withheld Us from him.*
>
> 69:44-7

He felt himself surrounded by celestial guardians, attentive observers of his attitude towards his mission:

> *Except a messenger whom He chooses. For surely He makes a guard to go before him and after him that He may know that they have truly delivered the messages of their Lord …*
>
> 72:27-8

It is not true that the Qur'an reflects the personality of the Prophet. Far from it. Most of the time it passes him by in silence, and treats him as a total abstraction. When it does mention him, it does so to judge, direct or dominate him.

His joys and daily sufferings – the deep grief he felt at the death of his children or friends, the Year of Mourning in which he lost his wife and uncle and with them all the moral support which had sustained him during his preaching campaign – do we see the slightest echo of these in the Qur'an? But as soon as his life is concerned with a matter of moral conduct, we see him in the grips of its legislative authority, as a subjected soul, the one often opposing itself to the other as intransigence versus clemency, extreme frankness versus timidity, patience versus impatience.

And it is not rare for Qur'anic teachings to contain severe reproaches for the slightest deviation on the part of the Prophet in relation to the ideal proposed:[3]

> *It is not fit for a prophet to take captives unless he has fought and triumphed in the land. You desire the frail goods of this world, while Allāh desires (for you) the Hereafter …*
>
> 8:67-8

> *Allāh pardon thee! Why didst thou permit them until those who spoke the truth had become manifest to thee and thou hadst known the liars?*
>
> 9:43

> *It is not for the Prophet and those who believe to ask forgiveness for the polytheists, even though they should be near relatives, after it has become clear to them that they are companions of the flaming fire.*
>
> 9:113

> *He frowned and turned away, because the blind man came to him. And what would make thee know that he might purify himself, or be mindful, so the Reminder should profit him?*
>
> 80:1-4

As soon as he is not in possession of an order or a precise teaching from this Source, the Muhammad we see in the Qur'an is by nature timid:

> *… Surely this gives the Prophet trouble, but he forbears from you …*
>
> 33:53

sensitive to what is being said of him:

> *… and thou fearedst men, and Allāh has a greater right that thou shouldst fear Him …*
>
> 33:37

hesitant, consulting his companions about matters:

> *… So pardon them and ask protection for them, and consult them in (important) matters …*
>
> 3:158

observing complete abstention in matters of the slightest doubt:

O Prophet, why dost thou forbid (thyself) that which Allāh has made lawful for thee? Seekest thou to please thy wives?

66:1

avowing ignorance of his own destiny, as of those of others:

Say: I know not whether that which you are promised is nigh or if my Lord will appoint for it a distant term.

72:25

Say: I am not the first of the messengers, and I know not what will be done with me or with you. I follow naught but that which is revealed to me …

46:9

But as soon as Muhammad is illuminated by this mysterious voice, he transmits this Message with the authority of a master whom nothing in the world can bring down. He takes on the role of universal precepter, for the instructed as much as for the ignorant:

… And say to those who have been given the Book and the Unlearned (people): Do you submit yourselves? If they submit, then indeed they follow the right way; and if they turn back, thy duty is only to deliver the message

3:19

Long before the Hijra, the Prophet declares it an essential part of his mission to bring enlightenment to the people of Israel, and to all the nations who had already received a Divine message. He is charged with telling them the truth on the subjects of their disputes:

And We have not revealed to thee the Book except that thou mayest make clear to them that wherein they differ…

16:64

Surely this Qur'ān declares to the Children of Israel most of that wherein they differ.

27:76

In pronouncing his judgements, he never beats about the bush. Direct, with a firm and undeviating step, he cleaves and decides:

… be steadfast as thou art commanded, and follow not their low desires, and say: I believe in what Allāh has revealed of the Book, and I am commanded to do justice between you …

42:15

In this disengaged, decisive attitude we see no trace of mere eclecticism, nor of cold, calculating intelligence, capable of today rejecting what it adopted yesterday, tomorrow demolishing what it built today. Beyond his unbending resolve we easily discern a force quite other than that of personality. That is why the Prophet shows an imperturbable countenance in the face of the powers of the world, and throughout the crucial hours of his life, absolutely confident of the Divine presence and His solicitude:

> *... he said to his companion: Grieve not, surely Allāh is with us ...*
>
> 9:40

That is why, while the sceptics retreat, the Prophet, infinitely sure of the divinity of his mission, voluntarily exposes himself and those close to him to the consequences of the *mubāhala* (ordeal), that solemn prayer when the chastisement of God is called down upon liars:[4]

> *... then let us be earnest in prayer, and invoke the curse of Allāh on the liars.*
>
> 3:60

Thus it is that, in the presence of an infinite number of sufficiently tangible proofs, Christian seekers of impartial truth recognize in the Arab Prophet a sincerity which is both communicative and psychologically extremely convincing.[5]

It could be argued, however, that this psychologically convincing sincerity is not necessarily the result of true veracity, or the active Power behind the revelations. The inspired person could, in fact, be the victim of unconscious illusion: he could suddenly see ideas and expressions he believes to be totally new surging into his spirit, when in reality he is doing no more than remixing old material that has lain dormant and forgotten in his soul; newly acquired knowledge could seem in his eyes to be the stuff of inspiration, give rise in him to the same conviction as his personal inspirations, without him giving attention to their true origin.

But these illusions and weaknesses of memory are symptomatic of a more or less abnormal mental state. From the double aspect of both subject and object, this is far from applicable in the present case.

From the point of view of the object, therefore, and inasmuch as history can enlighten us on this point, we would be dealing either with a work derived from popular sources or with vague and contradictory rumours. But neither of these can explain the single-minded integrity of the line taken by the Qur'an, or its trenchant and decisive progression.

As for the subject, there is no indication that Muhammad suffered from the slightest mental failing. Quite the contrary. We can do no better here than to record the statement of Renan (without, however, adopting his conclusion):[6]

> Never was a head more lucid than his; never did a man have better command over his thought than he.

It is true that subjectivity is unable to distinguish between the state of waking and of sleeping: dreaming or awake, one is equally convinced that one is exercising one's senses and being confronted by reality. But it is through the confrontation of the facts of the two systems, by the degree of their concordance or discordance, that one can judge with certitude their objectivity.

Having had experience of the two states, Muhammad speaks to us, wide awake, of his double contact with the visible and the invisible, with matter and spirit. For him it was an experience that he lived, a thousand times repeated and verified. Not only did he hear in all clarity the word of God as revealed, but he saw it with his own eyes; sharply, in its majestic form:

> *Surely it is the word of a bountiful Messenger, the possessor of strength, established in the presence of the Lord of the Throne, one (to be) obeyed, and faithful. And your companion is not mad. And truly he saw himself on the clear horizon. Nor is he niggardly of the unseen. Nor is it the word of an accursed devil.*
>
> 81:19-25

and several times:

> *By the star when it sets! Your companion errs not, nor does he deviate. Nor does he speak out of desire. It is naught but revelation that is revealed – One Mighty in Power has taught him, the Lord of Strength. So he attained to perfection, and he is in the highest part of the horizon. Then he drew near, drew nearer yet, so he was the measure of two bows or closer still ... Do you then dispute with him as to what he saw?*
>
> 53:1-12

How, indeed, can one contest a man healthy in body and spirit *as to what he saw*?

To be sure, we spectators cannot reconstruct the experience of the subject and live what he has lived. However, we do have a means of verification to help us realize whether we are dealing with hallucinatory exaltation, a pathological phenomenon 'with which solitary superhumans are struck',[7] or whether it is the very voice of truth which inspires him. To do this, we must not investigate his affirmation and his conviction, but the very content of his teaching.

Here then are three samples:

1) religious, moral and historical truths

We have been able to see by the example of moral precept that neither a personal enthusiasm, nor a vague and indirect knowledge of the holy Books, would have been capable on their own of assuring that the Arab Prophet would be in perfect concordance with his predessors.

One could suggest that he constantly had the Biblical text before his eyes, or that he had learned it by heart, in order to have drawn upon the necessary teaching for each occasion:

> *And thus do We repeat the messages, and that they may say, Thou hast studied; and that We may make it clear to a people who know.*
>
> 6:106

Besides its essential identity, we have also noted an independence of tone and manner in the presentation of the Qur'anic lessons. It would be of great interest to establish an analogous parallelism in the subjects of Divine attributes, angels, prophets, or life after death ... but this goes beyond the restricted framework of our *Introduction*.

Let us content ourselves by saying that, where the two religious monuments, the Bible and the Qur'an, treat the same subject matter,[8] the common foundation bespeaks itself in a striking identity, with differences only in certain secondary details. Most of the time, the Qur'anic exposé is distinguished by its sobriety, and its more accentuated orientation on the side of the religious lesson to be derived from each recitation. In his 'Analogies et Divergences entre les Légendes de la Bible et du Koran', Jules David was able to write:[9]

> The foundation is the same, the differences only in form, or certain insignificant details.

We shall not label as divergences certain additions or omissions, silences here, more or less developed mentions there. In our eyes, what is deserving of this name are the oppositions and contradictions. Such divergences thus defined are extremely rare and often wide open to interpretation.

The sceptics fixate on certain trifling differences, on the grounds of which they reject everything else, but logic demands of us a very different attitude. While accepting the sincerity of all the reporters worthy of credit, we must stop at the divergent points, either to suspend judgement, or to look for an order of importance which would lead us to lay more credence on one than another.

The same procedure which is used to reconcile, or arrange in a hierarchy, the four Gospels, should be applied to the ensembled religious heritage which the messengers of God have left us. All, for us, are saintly and holy. In spite of the distance which separates them in time and space, in spite of their differences in language and racial source, they are evidence of the same experience of the Divine. The concordance of their testimony about what is essential should open the eyes of the profane to the truth of the teachings which describe to us the true nature of the supreme Reality under its various aspects.

2) scientific truths

But, in its exhortations to faith and virtue, the Qur'an does not draw its lessons from traditional teachings and past events alone. It also points to permanent cosmological events: it calls our attention to the positive, immovable laws, not simply for their own interest, but with the aim of bringing the Creator to mind. We would maintain that the formulations describing them correspond exactly with the most up-to-date information held by the sciences.

Such, for example, as the innermost source whence the generative element of our being spurts forth:

> *He is created of water pouring forth, coming from between the back and the ribs.*
>
> 86:6-7

the different phases of our formation within the mother:

> *... We created you from dust, then from a small life-germ, then from a clot, then from a lump of flesh, complete in make and incomplete, that We may make clear to you. And We cause what We please to remain in the wombs till an appointed time, then We bring you forth as babies, then that you may attain your maturity ...*
>
> 22:5

> *And certainly We create man of an extract of clay, then We make him a small life-germ in a firm resting-place, then We make the life-germ a clot, then We make the clot a lump of flesh, then We make (in) the lump of flesh bones, then We clothe the bones with flesh, then We cause it to grow into another creation ...*
>
> 23:12-14

the number of shadowy hollows in the depth of which this creation is brought about:

> *He created you from a single being, then made its mate of the same (kind) … He creates you in the wombs of your mothers – creation after creation – in triple darkness …*
>
> 39:6

the aquatic origin of all living beings:

> *… And We made from water everything living …*
>
> 21:30

the formation of rain:

> *Allāh is He Who sends forth the winds, so they raise a cloud, then He spreads it forth in the sky as He pleases, and He breaks it, so that you see the rain coming forth from inside it …*
>
> 30:48

the cycles of the heavens and the earth:

> *… He makes the night cover the day and makes the day overtake the night, and He has made the sun and the moon subservient; each one moves on to an assigned term …*
>
> 39:5

the sphericity of the latter being incomplete towards the poles:

> *See they not that We are visiting the land, curtailing it of its sides …*
>
> 13:41; 21:44

how the course of the sun runs toward its apogee:

> *And the sun moves on to its destination …*
>
> 36:38

the fashion in which animal societies in general live in a collectivity no less coherent than human communities:

> *And there is no animal in the earth, nor a bird that flies on its two wings, but (they are) communities like yourselves …*
>
> 6:38

the description of the life of bees in particular:

> *And thy Lord revealed to the bee: Make hives in the mountains and in the trees and in what they build, then eat of all the fruits and walk in the ways of thy Lord submissively. There comes forth from their bellies a beverage of many hues, in which there is healing for men ...*
>
> 16:68-9

the duality of sex in plants and other creatures of the world:

> *Glory be to Him Who created pairs of all things, of what the earth grows, and of their kind and of what they know not!*
>
> 36:36

> *And of everything We have created pairs that you may be mindful.*
>
> 51:49

fertilization by the wind:

> *And We sent the winds fertilizing ...*
>
> 15:22

and so on.[10]

3) prevision

Beyond these established truths, the Qur'an also announces events to come. We see these take place punctually as predicted.

Thus the Qur'an foretold the three changes of attitude of its adversaries (first unfavourable, then conciliatory, and finally hostile) and the successive vicissitudes which they would experience in line with their attitude (famine, prosperity and then defeat):

> *So wait for the day when the heaven brings a clear drought, enveloping men. This is a painful chastisement. Our Lord, remove from us the chastisement – surely we are believers. When will they be reminded? And a Messenger has indeed come, making clear; yet they turned away from him and said: One taught (by others), a madman! We shall remove the chastisement a little, (but) you will surely return (to evil).*
>
> 44:10-15

This defeat, which they would experience at Badr in the second year of the Hijra, was announced several years before the Hijra and was to take place simultaneously with that of the Persians by the Romans:

The Romans are vanquished in a near land, and they, after their defeat, will gain victory ... And on that day the believers will rejoice in Allāh's help ...
30:2-5

One particularly curious fact about this battle, predicted right at the inception of Islam, was the sabre-blow that Walīd bin al-Mughīra would receive on his nose, leaving a scar to cause his compatriots hilarity for the rest of his life:

We shall brand him on the snout.
68:16

It is unnecessary for us to mention the desperate conditions in which the Qur'an affirmed not only its imminent triumph and the permanence of its doctrine:

... Then as for the scum, it passes away as a worthless thing; and as for that which does good to men, it tarries in the earth ...
13:17

but the immediate spread of the empire of youthful Islam over the world:

Allāh has promised to those of you who believe and do good that He will surely make them rulers in the earth as He made those before them rulers, and that He will surely establish for them their religion, which He has chosen for them, and that He will surely give them security in exchange after their fear ...
24:55

and the impotence of all the armies of the earth which would try to annihilate it:

Surely those who disbelieve spend their wealth to hinder (people) from the way of Allāh. So they will go on spending it, then it will be to them a regret, then they will be overcome ...
8:36

Moreover, it does not omit to foretell the future of each of the two religious communities which preceded it. Both the perpetual state of schism in Christianity:

And with those who say, We are Christians, We made a covenant, but they neglected a portion of that whereof they were reminded so We stirred up enmity and hatred among them to the day of Resurrection ...

5:14

and the dispersion of the Jews over the earth, their persecution in one place or another until the end of the world, and their constant need of an ally:

And when thy Lord declared that He would send against them to the day of Resurrection those who would subject them to severe torment ... And We divided them in the earth into parties ...

7:167-8

Abasement will be their lot wherever they are found, except under a covenant with Allāh and a covenant with men ...

3:111

Also the superiority of the Christians over the Jews right up to the day of Resurrection:

When Allāh said: O Jesus, I will ... clear thee of those who disbelieve ... to the day of Resurrection ...

3:54

and many other instances.[11]

So, past, present, future, all in the order of reality adapts to and confirms the world of ideas. What should one conclude from this? Either that both are one, or that there is a pact with providence, and it watched over the giving out of teaching to safeguard it from all error, or that God is deceiving us and giving all the signs of truth to shine in favour of a liar, without giving us the necessary light to uncover his imposture.

But the value of the Qur'an is not only in what it says, it is also in what it abstains from and in what it omits to say. Beyond the science which it reveals it places a zone which is off bounds, impenetrable to our enquiries, reserved for Divine knowledge alone. Has anyone ever succeeded in penetrating it with sure steps? X-rays are discovered in vain, they are still powerless to unveil for us with absolute certainty the form, colour and sex of a child in the depths of its mother:

... He knows what is in the wombs ...

31:34

However many meteorological offices we set up, their predictions always remain in the realm of probability. And what is the soul? The final word of philosophy on this subject has been, and will always remain, What do I know?:

And they ask thee about the revelation. Say: the revelation is by the commandment of my Lord, and of knowledge you are given but a little.

17:85

It is not enough to say that the Qur'an is an encyclopaedia of the knowledge of its times. All times have their illusions which they hold to be definitive truths, whose errors are not established until afterwards, but in its trajectory across knowledge, the Qur'an does not falter. The truths which it advances are, and will always be, unbeatable and unbeaten:

Falsehood cannot come at it from before or behind it …

41:42

Not only does it not fall into the hereditary mistakes of antiquity or Arabia; at the same time it does not linger over mean, plain details which carry the terrestrial imprint of its environment.

In his *Berceau de l'Islam à la Veille de l'Hégire*, Lammens expresses regret that the Book did not furnish any usable details that would help in the description of the climate or weather of its country, while it goes into ecstasies over the stars, the mountains, the clouds and other ordinary phenomena whose marvels it points out.[12]

But this is, in our opinion, proof that the Qur'an is not simply a local work. The truths which it teaches are those which any person is capable of seizing and drawing moral benefit from. This is why it is exalted beyond geographical particularities, racial or otherwise. This is why it generally does not name the people and places of which it speaks, and only retains the lessons necessary to educate humanity. Its transcendent tone is a proof unique to itself.

Certainly Qur'anic doctrine took flight in Arabic and was diffused in the first place amongst Arabs, but it was destined for the whole universe:

… that he might be a warner to the nations.

25:1

It is naught but a Reminder to the nations.

38:87

And it is naught but a Reminder for the nations.

68:52

Notes

Preface

1 In the opinion of the translator, there is still no one completely satisfactory translation of the Qur'an into English, nor indeed can there be into any language, since it is untranslatable. The three translations most valued by English readers would appear to be: A.J. Arberry, *The Koran Interpreted* (Oxford, 1964), whose poetic quality and use of 'high English' capture the exaltation of the Qur'an's sacred language; Yusuf Ali, *The Holy Qur'an* (Lahore, 1975), which provides a useful, literal translation; N.J. Dawood, *The Koran* (Harmondsworth, 1956), which gives a sound overall view, a good sense of the interconnection between verses (often lacking in more literal translations), and gets to the heart of the logic behind a line of argument, even if precision sometimes suffers as a consequence.

For the purposes of this work, we have used the translations of Maulana Muhammad Ali, *The Holy Qur'ān, Arabic text, English translation and commentary* (Ohio, 1995).

Part One

Chapter One

1 It is known that the Prophet always refrained from tracing his genealogy beyond ʿAdnān; we even know that he accused those genealogists who ventured to do so of imposture. If we are to believe a tradition attributed to Ibn ʿAbbās [see al-Nabahānī, *Anwār al-Muḥammadiyya* (Beirut, 1312 AH), p 18], there were said to be '30 unknown generations' between ʿAdnān and Ismāʿīl; this would make Ismāʿīl the 51st ancestor of Muhammad. But since it is generally acknowledged that the era of Abraham was somewhere between the twentieth and eighteenth century BC, there would have to have been at least 2260 years between Ismāʿīl and ʿAbd Allāh, the father of Muhammad (supposing that Ismāʿīl was born in 1720 BC and ʿAbd Allāh in 540 BC). Now, it is clear that the 51 generations alluded to in this tradition could not have filled this interval, unless we allow 44 years for each generation (instead of 33 years, which is the average).

2 Although all are unanimous in designating a Monday in the second quarter, tradition hesitates between the 8th, 10th and 12th of the month. In his *Mémoire sur le Calendrier Arabe avant l'Islamisme* (Paris, 1858), p 38, the Egyptian astronomer

Mahmoud Pacha al-Falaki places the birth of the Prophet precisely at 9 Rabīʿ al-Awwal, which he calculates as corresponding with 20 April in the Julian calendar, in accordance with the opinion of Silvestre de Sacy.

If one is aware of the fact that, with the Arabs, the determination of the first day of the month does not generally follow the astronomical conjunction of the moon with the sun, nor even the possible visibility of the crescent, but depends upon a factor that varies considerably according to local meteorological conditions, that is, the first effective appearance of the crescent after sunset, one can easily understand the hesitation between these various dates on the part of the ancient biographers.

As to the correspondence between the lunar and solar dates, the French historian Caussin de Perceval gives us a rather different figure. Starting from the hypothesis that the Arab calendar had begun to fall out of phase some time before the Prophet's birth, and that this did not come to an end until the intervention of the latter, this eminent historian believes that he can demonstrate that the birth of the Prophet took place on 29 August 570 AD. See Caussin de Perceval, *Essai sur l'Histoire des Arabes* (Paris, 1847), Vol 1, p 283.

3 Ibn Hishām, *Sīrat al-Rusūl* (Cairo, 1929), Vol 1, p 115

4 The word *fuḍūl* signifies, literally, intervention by good works. This Meccan confederation aimed to uphold the weak, render justice to the oppressed, and assure intertribal peace against the attempts of anyone who tried to violate it.

5 Later, at Medina, the Prophet had another child, Ibrāhīm, by Mary the Copt. In his turn, the boy died several months before the death of his father. See al-Falaki, *Mémoire*, p 7.

6 Al-Bukhārī, *Kitāb al-Adab* (Cairo, 1239 AH), bk 18, relates two discussions on this subject, the first having as its proponent al-Aqraʿ bin Ḥābis. Seeing the Prophet embracing al-Ḥasan, his grandson, this man of the Tamīmī tribe made the following remark: 'I have ten children and I do not embrace one of them.' The Prophet replied, 'God does not show mercy to him who does not have it himself.'

In the second account, another Bedouin (probably Qays bin ʿĀṣṣim) cried, 'You embrace little children! We never do that.' To this the Prophet replied, 'What can I do for you, since God has deprived your heart of all human feeling?' See Perceval, *Essai*, Vol 3, p 336

7 Al-Bukhārī's version does not say how long this devotional retreat lasted. It is only stated that, in his isolation, Muhammad gave himself up to spiritual exercises for several nights, and whenever his provisions were exhausted he went to fetch replenishments from his family in town. Ibn Isḥāq maintains that this intermittent retreat lasted a month.

8 Note that the very tenor of these phrases, which constitute the first outpouring of the Qur'anic revelation, demonstrate sufficiently that it is announcing a form of knowledge not yet acquired, which is about to be imparted thanks to the bounty of the Creator. It is clear that the expression would have been quite different if this inspiration had been the end result of long and mature meditations, as some have tried to explain it.

9 *Nāmūs* means Divine law.

10 *Hijra* refers to emigration, or a voluntary withdrawal determined by involuntary causes. We know that at a certain point in his mid-career, Muhammad

had to go into exile, on the eve of a plot to be carried out on his life. He settled in Medina where he arrived at the beginning of Rabīᶜ al-Awwal (on the 2nd, 8th or 12th of the month, according to various writers. Relying on numerous documents, al-Falaki has pronounced his support for Monday the 8th, corresponding to 20 September 622 AD).

We must not forget, however, that the Muslim era takes its point of departure not from the very day of the Emigration, but from the lunar year in which this event took place, which began two months and several days before, on the first of Muḥarram (15 or 16 July 622). Given that the lunar year is only 355 days long, and that in consequence 33 lunar years are equivalent to roughly 32 solar years, the following formulae suffice in order to convert a Hijra date (H) into a Christian (C), or vice versa:

$$H + 622 - \frac{H}{33} = C \quad \text{and} \quad C - 622 + \frac{C-622}{32} = H$$

11 In an article entitled 'Age de Mohammed', *Journal Asiatique* Mar/April 1911, Père H. Lammens claims that the Prophet was younger by ten years, without giving any positive proof to support this claim. His only argument is that it seems extraordinary that a man having passed the age of 50 should have the energy required to create such a new existence.

On the admission of the Prophet himself: 'I was born during the time of the just reign of Chosroes. When Chosroes perished there was no Caesar after him.' Against the authentic testimony of his companions, Muᶜāwiya, Ibn ᶜAbbās and ᶜĀ'isha, and against the concordant historic facts found in the various annals, whether European, Persian or Hebrew, Lammens takes pleasure in opposing them with certain remarks collected from an anonymous work, plus certain contradictory apocryphal traditions, and ends by questioning not only this particular matter, but also the authenticity of the entire life of the Prophet and everything connected with it.

If we are to believe Lammens, dates, facts, personages and almost everything in the most authentic traditions are suspect, recorded according to predetermined calculations or by the demands of exegetic or lexicographic formulae or a desire for symmetry. Equally, the entire world of orientalism has been following a false path because of the Arab historians. Has knowledge much to gain from this negative, or might we even say, destructive, contribution?

What is more serious with Lammens is not only the humorous tone of his work, where at every step irony pierces through an irremediable, ill-founded scepticism, but also his impartiality in applying this Pyrrhonist attitude. No sooner is it a matter of an unfavourable opinion of the Prophet, be it even the most gratuitous or absurd, then his scepticism is transformed into a convinced certitude. Hence it is nothing less than a hostile *parti pris*, which does not blush to talk in the name of the critic, and against logic itself.

Chapter Two

1 In fact this order is not strict. There are some exceptions in each category, which means that a deeper reason behind the arrangement is discernible.

2 Thus the second *sūra* is the first after the *Fātiḥa* and is the longest in the book, taking up 40 pages in the average edition.

3 With the exception, perhaps, of the final verse of *Sūrat al-nisā'*, whose revelation a little before the death of the Prophet gave no indication to the Companions as to where it should be placed: they are said to have purely and simply added it to this *sūra* since it concerns a similar subject.

4 see Rustūfdūnī, *Tārīkh al-Qur'ān wa'l-Maṣṣāḥif* (1323 AH), pp 26-7

5 With this document in mind, Leblois has written: 'Who would not wish that, after the death of Jesus, one of his immediate disciples had not taken it upon himself to put down his teachings into writing?' [Leblois, *Le Koran et la Bible Hébraique*, p 47, n 5].

6 c.f. al-Zinjānī, *Tārīkh al-Qur'ān* (Cairo, 1935), p 17

7 c.f. al-Suyūṭī, *Itqān fī ʿUlūm al-Qur'ān* (Cairo, 1344 AH), Vol 1, p 58

8 Thus, for example, we find in Ibn Masʿūd's copy against the words of the text: (intermediate prayer), this explanation: = (the afternoon prayer), or: (which is the afternoon prayer).

We do not wish to discuss whether this definition is correct in itself, for the question is an extremely controversial one amongst the Companions. But, even admitting with al-Barā' that this definition was there in the early phase in place of the present phrase, and that it was later abrogated and replaced by the present one, it is never juxtaposed against it in the recited text – indicative of this very controversy over its interpretation.

Ibn al-Anbārī relates that during the course of the consolidation of the first recension, Ḥafṣa asked for the insertion of this explanatory phrase into the text; but since she could not attest to its authenticity her father, ʿUmar, categorically opposed her request [c.f. al-Suyūṭī, *Durr al-Manthūr* (Cairo, 1314 AH), Vol 1, p 303].

9 Thus we find in the recension of Ubayy, apart from the canonical *sūra*s, the two famous prayers called *qanūt*.

10 Apart from the personal copy belonging to ʿUthmān, most of the traditionalists are in accordance in saying that five manuscripts were destined for the following five towns: Mecca, Medina, Basra, Kufa and Damascus. But Abū Ḥātim al-Sijistānī mentions two other copies for the two provinces of Yemen and Bahrain [c.f. Ibn Abī Dāwūd, *Kitāb al-Maṣṣāḥif* (Cairo, 1936 AH), p 74].

11 For instance, the word *tābūt* which at Medina was written *tābūh* has kept its Meccan spelling.

12 Mālik, *Muwaṭṭa'* (Cairo, 1349 AH), Vol 1

13 Nöldeke, *Geschichte des Korans* (Leipzig, 1909-1938), Vol 2, p 93

14 c.f. Mirza Alexandre Kazem, *Journal Asiatique*, Dec 1843. The only difference, therefore, is in the way in which the Qur'an is divided into *sūra*s, and their numbering. Moreover, any more radical difference only exists in theory among these doctors. In fact, their copies differ in no way from those of the Sunnites. If there are certain mullahs fanatic enough to mention certain words supposed to have been omitted by ʿUthmān, they nonetheless do not allow themselves to insert them into their own copies, since they have not been sanctioned by the legitimate imam.

The same is true, and with even stronger reason, of the apocryphal passage which Garcin de Tassy published under the title of 'Observations sur le Chapitre Inconnu du Koran' [*Journal Asiatique*, Jul/Aug 1904], whose 'trial' Mirza Alexandre Kazem has undertaken. This scholar has shown in fact that not only is this so-called *sūra* not traceable in the Qur'ans of the Shīʿites, but that neither is there mention of it in their traditional polemic works. The very title, two lights, applied to Muhammad and ʿAlī, and according to Tūṣī did not appear among the Shīʿites earlier than the seventh century AH. Moreover, it suffices to read this piece, which is nothing more than a mediocre compilation of words and expressions taken from the Qur'an, to see the shocking contrast that it presents with the elegance and harmony of Qur'anic style. C.f. also Nöldeke, *Geschichte*, Vol 2, pp 107-112

15 Leblois, *Le Koran*, p 54

16 Muir, *Life of Mahomet*, cited in Barthélemy-St.-Hilaire, *Mahomet et le Koran* (Paris, 1865), p 33

17 Does the word *sabʿa* here really signify the number seven? Or does it mean an indeterminate number, a multitude? The question is controversial. Whatever the case may be, these 'seven readings' should not be confused with the 'seven readers' chosen by Ibn Mujāhid. There is no reason, either, to bring these two groups into correspondence, as Jeffrey suggests in the Arabic preface of the *Maṣṣāḥif*, p 8. In any case, Ibn Mujāhid was often reproached for his choice of seven [c.f. al-Suyūṭī, *Itqān*, p 49; Nöldeke, *Geschichte*, p 50; Ṭāhir, *Ṭibyān li-baʿḍ al-Mubāḥith al-Mutaʿallaqa bi'l-Qur'ān* (Cairo, 1934), p 81], as being susceptible to making people believe that every reading attributed to these authorities would be considered as canonical and vice versa; thus, only a methodical critique is capable of unravelling the true from the false. Contrary to the opinion of Jeffrey (ibid) this critique should be applied consistently to the Seven, the Ten, the Fourteen and every other source of variant.

18 al-Suyūṭī, *Itqān*, Vol 1, p 57

19 c.f. al-Suyūṭī, *Itqān*, p 50; Baqillānī, *Intiṣṣār*, quoted by Ṭāhir, *Tibyān*, p 73

20 c.f. al-Suyūṭī, *Itqān*, p 50; Ibn Ḥajar, quoted by al-Zinjānī, *Tārīkh*, p 44

21 Ibn Abī Dāwūd, *Maṣṣāḥif*, p 36

22 c.f. al-Zinjānī, *Tārīkh*, p 16

23 c.f. Ṭāhir, *Tibyān*, pp 39-40; Ibn Abī Dāwūd (*Maṣṣāḥif*, p 54) expresses the same opinion.

24 Jeffrey, 'Introduction', in Ibn Abī Dāwūd, *Maṣṣāḥif*, p 1

25 Jeffrey, 'Introduction', pp 9-10

26 Jeffrey, 'Introduction', p 6

27 c.f. Jeffrey, 'Introduction', compare p 5 with p 7

28 c.f. Jeffrey, 'Introduction', compare p 6 with p 212

29 Jeffrey, 'Introduction', p 8

30 c.f. Jeffrey, 'Introduction', compare p 8 with p 21

31 Jeffrey, 'Introduction', p x; p 9; p 23

32 Jeffrey, 'Introduction', p 8

33 c.f. al-Bukhārī, *Kitāb Faḍā'il al-Qur'ān*, bk 3; Ibn Abī Dāwūd, *Maṣṣāḥif*, p 25

34 Nöldeke, *Geschichte*, Vol 2, p 91

35 Jeffrey, 'Introduction', p 15

36 Jeffrey, 'Introduction', p 15

37 Take, for example, the so-called codex of Ibn Masʿūd. On this subject Ibn Isḥāq (cited by Jeffrey, 'Introduction', p 23, n) tells us that of the numerous copies of this codex, no two were identical. Similarly, Ibn al-Nadīm, *Fihrist* (1872), says that, contrary to what has often been said, he saw one such copy where the first *sūra* was to be found.

38 Jeffrey, 'Introduction', p 24

39 c.f. Ibn Abī Dāwūd, *Maṣṣāḥif*, p 35

40 Ibn Abī Dāwūd, *Maṣṣāḥif*, p 18

41 c.f. Schwally, in Nöldeke, *Geschichte*, Vol 2, p 92

42 see above, the case of ʿUmar, p 16, and that of Ḥafṣa, p 142

43 What is more, he did not do it on his own initiative, or without consulting the people. In a discourse recognized by critics of *ḥadīth* as authentic, and where the piety of the third caliph is strongly defended by his successor, he declared that this rigorous measure was taken by common agreement with all the Companions present. 'If ʿUthmān had not done it,' ʿAlī adds, 'I myself would have done it.' [c.f. Ibn Abī Dāwūd, *Maṣṣāḥif*, p 12, p 22]

Chapter Three

1 In order better to grasp the contrast between this revolution and other historical conquests, one would do well to read: Jouguet, *L'Impérialisme Macédonien et l'Hellénisation de l'Orient* (Paris, 1926) and Gautier, *Moeurs et Coutumes des Musulmans* (Paris, 1931), Vol 3.

2 Lammens, *Berceau de l'Islam à la Veille de l'Hégire* (Rome, 1914), p 265

3 Qur'an 59:8

4 Thus he showed mercy to the Qurayshite emissary who came to assassinate him after Badr; to the Jewish woman who tried to poison him at Khaybar; to another who, during the Emigration, brutally jostled his eldest daughter, Zaynab, then pregnant, causing her to miscarry. We see this indulgence in the way he treated those who sought to defame his innocent wife, ʿĀ'isha. One admires above all his infinitely pacific and generous conduct during and after the conquest of Mecca [c.f. Barthélemy-St.-Hilaire, *Mahomet*, pp 125-130].

5 c.f. Lammens, *Berceau*, p 247

6 We know that at the time of their exile the Muslims had left their property and riches in the hands of their persecutors:

> *Those who are driven from their homes without a just cause …*
>
> 22:40

We could, then, surely, allow them the right to partially indemnify themselves through the merchandise of the latter. This is what Saint-Clair Tisdall calls the expeditions for pillage [*Original Sources of the Qur'an* (London, 1905), p 276].

7 The changing of this authorization into a commandment occurred in conditions so unfavourable that one cannot see one's way to affirming with Saint-Clair Tisdall that 'Qur'anic law was modified proportionately to the military successes of Muhammad' [*Sources*, p 279]. The author has made other mistakes in the same chapter, firstly in reversing the sense of Qur'an 2:217 which condemns all hostility

during the sacred month [c.f. *Sources*, p 276] and secondly by taking the means of repression instituted against the terrorists:

> *The only punishment of those who wage war against Allāh and His Messenger and strive to make mischief in the land is that they should be murdered, or crucified, or their hands and their feet should be cut off on opposite sides, or they should be imprisoned ...*
>
> 5:33

for a new form of warfare, constituting a third stage in this evolution [c.f. *Sources*, p 277].

8 Having arrived thus far, and having systematically omitted to mention passages limiting the right to have recourse to force, Saint-Clair Tisdall is obliged, in order to measure with his conclusions, to replace this verse, which talks of the order to give hospitable protection to neutrals, by omission points.

9 see Draz, *La Morale du Koran*, chapters 2, 4 and 5

10 However, if it were really a matter of fighting against a religion, would it not be the religious person who would have to be chosen as a target?

11 c.f. Gautier, *Moeurs et Coutumes des Musulmanes* (Paris, 1931), p 209

12 Gautier, *Moeurs*

13 The author doubtless alludes to land taxes. In fact, historians report that the caliphs held great store by the fact that these taxes should be much less heavy for the native peoples than for the conquering Muslims. Thus, for example, ʿUmar II ordered the Governor of Egypt to impose on each Muslim property-owner 40 dinars and on each Copt property-owner 20 dinars [c.f. Ibn Tāghrībirdī, *Nujūm al-Zāhira*, Vol 1, p 238, cited by Salāma, *Enseignement Islamique en Egypte* (Cairo, 1939), p xiv]

14 Gautier, *Moeurs*, p 217

15 Gautier, *Moeurs*, p 207

16 Gautier, *Moeurs*, p 208

17 According to the most recent statistics (1983), even at their most modest, the Muslim world now accounts for one quarter of the total population.

18 Porter, 'Discours Préliminaire sur la Religion des Mahométans' (French translation), in Du Ryer, *Al-Coran*, Preface

Part Two

Chapter Four

1 c.f. Qur'an 2:133 and 3:84

2 Qur'an 30:30

3 Matt. 16:1-4

4 Qur'an 20:20

5 c.f. Matt. 12:28:

> I cast out devils by the Spirit of God

6 Qur'an 17:49

7 Qur'an 34:7
8 Qur'an 44:36
9 Qur'an 45:35
10 read, for example, *sūras* 13, 20, 39, 40, 41, 42, or passages like 2:255-260, 3:190-195, 4:77-79, 5:109-end, 6:95-104, 58:7, 59:21-end

Chapter Five

1 This position is held by an infinitely small minority of oral commentators, whose historicity is doubtful, as is the precise sense of their doctrine [al-Rāzī, *Mafātīḥ al-Ghayb, al-maᶜrūf bi'l-Tafsīr al-Qur'ān* (Cairo, 1278 AH), Vol 1, p 407]. In origin the verb *arja'a*, a term taken from the Qur'an (c.f. Qur'an 9:106) means 'not to prejudge the future destiny of Man', and 'to give oneself up to God's decision'. This does not prevent one from judging oneself and judging others according to their conduct here on earth. To go from there and say that everything depends upon faith and that nothing else can nullify it is taking a great step, because this would not only be prejudging, in another way, but also preaching at the same time against any moral or social law.

We know that, although they abstained from making judgements on religious controversies and political conflicts, certain Murji'ites rose up against the injustice of al-Hajjāj [Ibn Saᶜd, *Ṭabaqāt* (Leiden, 1335 AH), Vol 6, p 205]. On the other hand, we know that a man like Ibn Sirīn, well-known for his extremely indulgent abstention from (criticizing) other believers, was extremely severe as regards his own conduct [al-Nawawī, *Tahdhīb al-Asmā' wa'l-Lughāt* (London, 1847), p 108].

2 for this, consult the appendix of Draz, *La Morale*
3 Qur'an 7:157
4 Qur'an 16:90
5 Qur'an 7:28
6 Qur'an 7:33
7 see Draz, *La Morale*, ch 3, para 3
8 see also, among others, Qur'an 3:186, 42:40-3
9 Lev. 29:17-18
10 Abū Dāwūd, *Kitāb al-Ṭalāq*, bk 3
11 Ibn Saᶜd and Ḥākim, cited by al-Suyūṭī, *Jāmiᶜ al-Saghīr* (Cairo, 1350 AH), article '*Innamā*'
12 Gautier, *Moeurs*, p 216
13 Gaudefroy-Demombynes, 'L'Islam', in *Histoire et Historiens depuis Cinquante Ans* (1876-1926), p 739
14 Here Goldziher commits a contradiction in translating this verse thus: 'If you fear betrayal on the part of a people, pay them back with the same' [*Le Dogme et la Loi d'Islam* (Paris, 1920), p 23]. Kasimirsky makes the same error: 'render him the same', similarly Savary: 'treat them as they have acted'. It suffices to read the sequence of the verses to realize the incompatibility of this interpretation in the context.

Chapter Six

1 see al-Bukhārī, *Jāmiʿ al-Ṣaḥīḥ* (Cairo, 1289 AH), 'Kitāb Jihād', bk 101. See also Barthélemy-St.-Hilaire, *Mahomet*, pp 150-1

2 With rare exceptions, for sometimes the appearance of a pause is only kept up in stages and varies from one group of verses to another in the same chapter, e.g. *sūra*s 69 et seq.

3 In a preceding study in Arabic (*al-Naba' al-ʿAẓīm*) – whose publication in Cairo was suspended by our departure for France in 1936 – we have inspected certain characteristics of the Qur'anic style and shown, by concrete examples, what these particularities are. Here we do no more than summarize the essential points of this earlier work.

Quite apart from the commentaries and introductions to the Qur'an, numerous other specialized treatises have been devoted to this same task. May we cite among others: al-ʿAskarī, *Ṣināʿatayn* (Istanbul, 1320 AH); al-Jurjānī, *Dalā'il al-Iʿjāz*, and *Asrār al-Balāgha* (Cairo, 1912 and 1925); al-Baqillānī, *Iʿjāz al-Qur'ān* (Cairo, 1915). Among contemporary writers we should above all mention al-Rāfiʿī, *Iʿjāz al-Qur'ān wa'l-Balāgha al-Nabawiyya* (Cairo, 1928). More recently, Kamil Hussein in 1936 made a study on the form of the Qur'an, of which there is a typed copy in the Massignon Library.

4 Abū'l-Ḥassan Ibrāhīm bin ʿUmar al-Biqāʿī, a Shāfiʿī of the ninth century AH, master of al-Suyūṭī. The latter devoted a chapter of his *Itqān* to this subject [Vol 2, p 108].

5 Qur'an 46:1

6 Qur'an 74:2

7 Qur'an 26:214

8 Qur'an 28:59

9 Qur'an 6:93

10 Qur'an 21:107

11 Qur'an 2:219

12 Qur'an 5:90

13 Qur'an 4:77

14 Qur'an 2:190

Part Three

Chapter Seven

1 Renan, 'Mahomet et les Origines de l'Islamisme' in *Revue des Deux Mondes*, 15 December 1851

2 Renan, 'Mahomet', pp 1070-1

3 Renan, 'Mahomet', p 1089

4 Qur'an 3:163, 62:2

5 Qur'an 33:33, 48:26

6 Renan, 'Mahomet', p 1090

7 see Ibn Hishām, *Sīrat al-Rusūl*, Vol 1, p 144

8 Renan, 'Mahomet', p 1090

9 '*maṭarnā bi-najmin kadhā*': al-Bukhārī, *Ṣaḥīḥ*, 'Kitāb Maghāzī', bk 37

10 see Part 2, ch 4 above
11 see Part 2, ch 4 above
12 c.f. Sale, 'Observations Historiques et Critiques sur le Mahométisme', in Du Ryer, *Al-Coran*, pp 30-1
13 see article 'Sabia', *Encyclopaedia of Islam*
14 see in Huart ['Une Nouvelle Source du Koran' in *Journal Asiatique*, Jul/Aug 1904, p 127] the following conclusion: 'the Arabic texts which have been discovered, published and studied since then do not allow us to see in the role attributed to this Syrian monk anything other than fantasy.'
15 Massé, *L'Islam* (Paris, 1937), p 21
16 Huart, 'Source', p 131
17 Lammens, *L'Islam, Croyance et Institutions* (Beirut, 1926), p 28
18 Goldziher, *Dogme*, p 4
19 Andrae, *Mahomet, sa Vie et sa Doctrine* (Paris, 1945), pp 37-8
20 Sprenger, cited by Huart, 'Source', p 128
21 see Sale, *Observations*, pp 68-71
22 Taylor, Isaac, *Ancient Christianity*, Vol 1, p 266
23 Taylor, cited by Saint-Clair Tisdall, *Sources*, pp 136-7
24 ibid.
25 see Massé, *L'Islam*, p 17
26 Nöldeke, *Geschichte*, p 10. See also Zamakhsharī on Qur'an 5:5.
27 Huart, 'Source', p 129
28 Qur'an 29:48
29 Saint-Clair Tisdall in fact goes as far as maintaining that certain Islamic notions derive from Zoroastrianism, and devotes an entire chapter to the elements he says are Zoroastrian in the Qur'an and Sunna. Without prejudging anything of the origins or even the parentage of the ideas mentioned by him under this title, we would maintain that, apart from the idea of the houris, these elements do not even form part of the Qur'an itself. They belong to certain traditions to a lesser or greater degree doubtful in their authenticity, for instance ideas about the Light of Muhammad, the angel of death, Azrael, the bridge of death mentioned in the *Sīra*, etc.
30 This interpretation is absurd in certain passages, contradictory in others, like where the word *ummī* is applied to the uneducated Jews. When the Prophet says of himself and his people, 'We are an unlettered (illiterate) people,' he explains it in these terms: 'We do not write, and neither do we calculate.' [al-Bukhārī, *Saḥīḥ*, 'Kitāb al-Ṣawm', bk 13]
31 see, for example, Leblois, *Le Koran*, p 34. Following the example of the others, Leblois has tried to prove the opposite with a tradition according to which the Prophet, on his deathbed, asked for writing materials to be brought to him so that he could write his will regarding the succession of the caliphate.

But the argument proves nothing: it does not say that the Prophet wrote; one can conclude nothing from the unrealized undertaking of a dying man; the verb 'to write' attributed to the great leaders in general (even more so in the case of a leader known amongst his disciples for never having held a pen in his hand nor deciphered any writing) signifies nothing more than to dictate and affix one's seal or mark. Thus in discussing his diplomatic correspondence the term *kataba ilā fulān* is used to signify 'through the intermediary of his secretaries'. Likewise, for the treaty of Ḥudaybiyya it is said *bayna-mā yaktubu huwa wa-Suhayl idh ṭalaʿa* … , when it was ʿAlī, at the dictation of the Prophet, who put it into writing.

People have tried to draw another argument from an episode linked with this same treaty: ʿAlī having entitled the treaty 'Peace Treaty between Muhammad, Messenger of God and … ', the Qurayshite delegate objected that, if he recognized Muhammad's title as the Messenger of God, he would not have fought against him in the first place. Accepting this, the Prophet ordered his title to be effaced, but the pious secretary did not dare to acquiesce. So the Prophet asked him where the word was that should be crossed out, and rubbed it out with his own hand. So far there are no difficulties. Except that one very concise and elliptical version adds '… and wrote in its place: Muhammad son of ʿAbd Allāh'. Which apparently imputes the ability to write to the Prophet.

But this episode is not really problematical: on the one hand the general rule is that this attribution be understood in the sense of the act being mediated; on the other hand, the apparent equivocation is elucidated in other versions, where it is stated precisely that once the first epithet was effaced by the Prophet's own hand, ʿAlī replaced it with the new one. To say from this ambiguity that the Prophet knew how to write would be too quickly to forget the fact that he was not able to recognize the word to be expunged, other than at the guidance of the scribe; what is more, it would be to close one's eyes to the explanation, given at this very juncture, for why recourse was made to a scribe – the Prophet 'did not know how to write': *lā yuḥsinu yaktub*.

So, as backed up by the Prophet himself (*mā ana bi-qāri': naḥnu ummatun ummiyya*), by his behaviour during his lifetime, by the testimony of his disciples, by the objections of his enemies, and finally by the solemn proclamation of the Qur'an, the illiteracy of Muhammad seems to us to be firmly established. All attempts to establish the opposite are too feeble to make an impact. Muhammad did not live on another planet: the details of his life are known to us in the smallest detail, and his people would not err through naive credulity. If the Prophet knew how to read would he not, at least on occasion, have looked at and verified his correspondence, or the copies of his Qur'an?

Thus, despite the ambiguity of certain accounts, Nöldeke arrived at the following conclusions: 1) that Muhammad himself called himself illiterate and that is why he had the Qur'an and his letters read for him, and; 2) that in any case he had not read the Bible or any other great work [*Geschichte*, Vol 1, p 16].

32 c.f. Leblois, *Le Koran*, p 35. Graf is yet more positive: it was only several centuries later that a Bible in the Arabic language made its appearance. Padwick states that it was only in the ninth and tenth centuries that any need was felt for an Arabic translation of the Gospel [Padwick, 'The Origin of Arabic Translations', in *Moslem World*, April 1939]. In spite of his indefatigable researches in various libraries, Chidiac says he has not been able to find any mention of the New Testament translated into Arabic prior to the eleventh century [Chidiac, *Etude sur*

Al-Ghazāli, Réfutation Exellente de la divinité du Jésus-Christ, d'après les Evangiles (Paris, 1933), ch 7].
33 see below, Part I, end of ch 2
34 Sprenger, *Das Leben und die Lehre des Mohammeds*, Vol 1, p 78, cited and developed by Huart, *Source*, p 133
35 c.f. Ibn Hishām, *Sīra*, Vol 1, p 183
36 Huart, *Source*, p 131

Chapter Eight
1 see Part I, ch 3
2 al-Bukhārī, *Ṣaḥīḥ*, 'Kitāb al-Ṣawm', bk 23
3 It is true that she was betrothed to him a little before the Hijra, but this is further proof that the principle which authorizes bigamy is ancient, not the effect of a new moral conception determined by the atmosphere of Medina.
4 Read the reports of ʿĀ'isha and other mothers of the believers on how he spent his nights. Dragging himself from sleep, he would abandon himself to prolonged prayer, sometimes standing until his feet became swollen [al-Bukhārī, *Ṣaḥīḥ*, 'Kitāb Tahajjud', bk 6] sometimes so prostrate that he seemed dead [al-Bayhaqī, quoted by Nabahānī, *Anwār*, p 522]; how sometimes he went to the cemetery to pray for the souls of the dead [Muslim, *Ṣaḥīḥ*, 'Kitāb Janāyiz', bk 35). Everything shows that the piety of the Prophet, far from diminishing, was confirmed and strengthened at Medina. The Prophet did not have need of being surrounded by pious and honest souls, not to transmit to us a considerable part of his tradition, and in particular the teaching directed to women, destined for one half of humanity, nor to complete the proof of his sincerity by their concordant witness of his depth of character in intimate life, where all the veils of social hypocrisy fall or are torn away.
5 Massé, *L'Islam*, p 21
6 Lammens, *L'Islam*, p 33
7 Andrae, *Mahomet*, p 139; see also Lammens, *L'Islam*, p 28
8 Gaudefroy-Demombynes, *Institutions Musulmanes* (Paris, 1946), p 66; Andrae, *Mahomet*, p 81
9 Andrae, *Mahomet*, p 137
10 Andrae, *Mahomet*, p 138
11 Gaudefroy-Demombynes, *Institutions*, p 68
12 Goldziher, *Dogme*, pp 21-2
13 To guide the reader in his consultation of the Qur'an at this point, we give here the references for the Meccan passages which deal with these stories: *Sūrat al-Aʿrāf*: Adam 11-25, Moses 102-176; *Sūrat Yūnus*: Moses 75-92; *Sūrat Hūd*: Noah 25-49, Abraham and Lot 69-82; *Sūrat Yūsuf*: Joseph, Adam, Abraham and Lot 26-77; *Sūrat Banī Isrā'īl*: The People of Israel 4-8; *Sūrat al-Kahf*: The Seven Sleepers 9-25, Moses 60-82; *Sūrat Maryam*: Zachariah, John the Baptist, Mary, Jesus, etc. 1-33; *Sūrat Ṭā Hā*: Moses 9-98; *Sūrat al-Anbiyā'*: Abraham 51-70, David, Solomon 78-82; *Sūrat al-Shuʿarā'*: Moses, Abraham, Noah, etc. 10-189; *Sūrat al-Naml*: Moses, David, Solomon 7-44; *Sūrat al-Qaṣaṣ*: Moses 3-43, Aaron 76-82; *Sūrat al ʿAnkabūt*:

Noah, Abraham, Lot 14-35; *Sūrat al-Saba'*: David, Solomon 10-14; *Sūrat Ṣād*: David, Solomon, Job 17-44; *Sūrat al-Dhāriyāt*: Abraham 24-37.

14 al-Bukhārī, *Ṣaḥīḥ*, 'Kitāb al-Ṣawm', bk 1, and Muslim, *Ṣaḥīḥ*, bk 19

15 Muslim, *Ṣaḥīḥ*, bk 36

16 a term originally equivocal, which signifies either rewriting, or annulment. In law and in terms of principle, it is used in the sense of abrogation, i.e. the cessation of the application of a provisional law.

Certain commentators extend the meaning of this word to include all kinds of illumination or precision brought to a previously unclear expression. Ibn Ḥazm used and abused the term in this context. It is not rare that in one and the same passage he takes the preposition 'apart from' or the conjunction 'but' for a *naskh* of the general term or of the opposite term which preceded it (see, for instance, 2:60, 196, 229, 233; 4:19, 22, 23, 146; 5:34; 29:60; 24:5; 25:70; 26:227; 60:8-9).

A striking example of his stretching the meaning of this term is found in his commentary on the well-known passage which comes at the beginning of the revelation:

> *O thou covering thyself up! Rise to pray by night except a little, half of it or lessen it a little, or add to it ...*
>
> 73:1-3

Except a little is, he says, *naskh* of *by night*; *half of it* is *naskh* of *except a little*; *lessen it* is *naskh* of *half of it*. Thus he finds three *naskh*s in a sole phrase, and he could have gone on.

If we count them all up according to Ibn Ḥazm's reckoning, is it astonishing that we find 224 places where *mansūkh* occur? Let us note, moreover, that he relates 114 of these 224 passages to the general idea of encouraging people (albeit from a distance) to withstand passively the aggression of the unfaithful – a transitional disposition as we know, which was replaced by the authorization to resist and to oppose force by force.

But what most deserves to be noticed here is the manner in which certain orientalists have transcribed these ideas. Seizing on this frightening figure, without taking into account the rather singular terminology of the author, they present it to us in rather an exaggerated manner, saying that is the number of Qur'anic contradictions recognized by the Muslims as having been determined by political changes [Renan, 'Mahomet', p 1079; see also Saint-Clair Tisdall, *Sources*, p 278]. This is a clear case of the gulf that can exist between words and realities.

17 Qur'an 18:9-25

18 Ibn Hishām, *Sīra*, Vol 1, pp 141-2; al-Bukhārī, *Ṣaḥīḥ*, 'Kitāb Hijra', bk 1

19 A similar anachronism, certainly with a wider time-gap, deserves to be pointed out in the supposed roles of Salmān the Persian and Mary the Copt as so-called initiators of Muhammad into the Zoroastrian and Christian faiths respectively.

Although he converted soon after the Hijra, Salmān remained a slave in the service of a despotic Jewish master for more than four years, and was not able to accompany the Prophet until the battle of Khandaq in the year 5 AH [Ibn Hishām, *Sīrat al-Rusūl*, pp 141-2]. Mary the Copt was to arrive even later, in the year 7 AH.

Is there any need to recall, furthermore, that even if the Qur'an could be linked with the Bible as members of the same family, there is a rupture between its doctrine and that of the Avesta?

20 al-Tirmidhī, *Jāmi*ᶜ (Cairo, 1292 AH), 'Kitāb Ṣifāt al-Qiyāma', bk 15

21 This is what the effort of Saint-Clair Tisdall in his *Sources* boils down to: in his avowed intention of showing that the Qur'an derives from legend rather than from history [*Sources*, pp 61-2], the author systematically ignores all the concordances with the Old and New Testaments, from the Creation until the end of the world, and dedicates himself exclusively to uncovering the parenthood of certain details in the Talmud and Judaeo-Christian traditions not contained in the Bible.

Conclusion

1 This judgement forms part of a very precious, historic Arabo-Roman document, little known in European annals, which describes an interrogation of the Qurayshite chief Abū Sufyān, conducted by the Emperor Heraclius. The interrogation is pithy, methodical, full of spirit and measure, and worthy of our recounting in full below.

In Syria, on his return from a victorious expedition to Persia in 628, the Roman Emperor found himself detained by a letter in which the Prophet called on him to embrace Islam. More surprised than importuned, and wanting to know more precisely what this communication could be about, the Emperor of Byzantium summoned some compatriots of this man so that he could interrogate them on the subject. Abū Sufyān, one of the most relentless adversaries of Muhammad, happened at that time to be in Syria, at the head of a group of Meccan merchants (this took place during the truce concluded between them and the Prophet in 6 AH). The emissary of Heraclius met the merchants and took them into the Counsel Chamber.

Abū Sufyān, being the most closely related to the Prophet of the group, underwent questioning, while his companions stood behind him in order to keep a watch on his answers and to eliminate, should the need arise, any possible lies. Abū Sufyān averred later that, if he had not been intimidated by the presence of his comrades, he would have slipped in some unfavourable insinuations about the Prophet; but restrained by shame, he had to declare the truth. When the questioning was over, Heraclius addressed the following reflections on what he had heard to his interpreter and told him to pass them on to Abū Sufyān:

'I asked you first about the family of this man, and you told me that he was of a good family. Now God always chooses his messengers from amongst the nobility of the people to which they belong.

'I asked you if anyone amongst you had used the kind of language he used before, and you said, 'No.' Then I thought to myself that if anyone before him had talked about the same things, I would have believed that he was doing no more than imitate his predecessors.

'Then I asked you further if, before he undertook this discourse, you ever suspected him of any lie, and you affirmed to the contrary. I understood by that that if he were not a man to lie regarding his own kind, he would not be capable, for even stronger reasons, of lying about God.

'I also asked you if any of his ancestors had ever been king, and you said, 'No.' Otherwise I would have said: this is a man who seeks to take back the throne of his fathers.

'I asked you if they were increasing or decreasing in number, and you answered that they were increasing. Now this is the property of faith, to increase up to its complete evolution.

'I asked you if anyone among them had reneged on his religion, and you said, 'No.' This is how it is with faith, when the grace of conviction in it penetrates the heart.

'Then I asked you if this man broke his promises, and you maintained the opposite. Thus it is with prophets: they do not betray.

'I asked you about the battles undertaken between you and him, and you said that sometimes he won and sometimes you did. Thus the prophets sometimes undergo trials, but final success is theirs.

'Finally I asked you about the nature of his commandments and you told me that he ordered you to renounce the beliefs of your fathers, to worship the sole God, to observe prayer, charity and chastity, faithfulness to promises made and the restitution of property entrusted to one's care.

'Now all this answers well to the picture of a true prophet. I knew well that such a man was going to appear, but I did not think that he would be one of you. If you have told the truth, it will be inevitable that this man will conquer the very place on which my feet are standing. As for myself, if I could get to him I would try very hard to meet him; if I were next to him, I would wash the dust from his feet.'

When Heraclius had finished speaking, Abū Sufyān relates, violent shouts were uttered by the important personages who surrounded him, and a great tumult arose. The emperor then gave the order that we should be led out ... From that time onwards, I remained humbly convinced of the imminent success of Muhammad [al-Bukhārī, *Ṣaḥīḥ*, 'Kitāb Jihād', bk 101].

2 The story of the defamatory incident that placed his family honour into the balance (*Ḥadīth al-Ifk*) is well known. A pronouncement was urgently needed, but revelation was awaited for a month – in the mean time he could not advance anything on the strength of his leadership either to confirm or confute the rumours. If the matter had depended on his own arbitration, would he not have been capable of shedding light on the situation by some show of eloquence, and even of attributing it to revelation?

3 If we examine the instances where the Qur'an complains about him, it is surprising to find in fact that they all relate to the one characeristic – the fact that, when confronted by two solutions equally permissible, and most often explicitly so, thus compare:

> *So when you meet in battle those who disbelieve, smite the necks; then, when you have overcome them, make (them) prisoners, and afterwards (set them free) as a favour or for ransom till the war lay down its burdens ...*
>
> 47:4

> *Only those are believers who believe in Allāh and His Messenger, and when they are with him on a momentous affair, they go not away until they have asked leave of him. Surely they who ask leave of thee, are they who believe in Allāh and His Messenger; so when they ask leave of thee for some affair of theirs, give leave to whom thou wilt of them ...*
>
> 24:62

> *Ask forgiveness for them or ask not forgiveness for them* ... cited above
>
> 9:79

> *Allāh has not made for any man two hearts within him nor has He made your wives whom you desert by Ẓihār, your mothers, nor has He made those whom you assert (to be your sons) your sons ...*
>
> 33:4

> *There is no harm for the Prophet in that which Allāh has ordained for him ...*
>
> 33:38

– the Prophet chose the one which he judged the best from the point of view of plain common sense, if not on its own merits:

> *Had they gone forth with you, they would have added to you naught but trouble, and would have hurried to and fro among you seeking (to sow) dissension among you. And among you there are those who would listen to them ...*
>
> 9:47

But in the eyes of Divine vision, such choices were not precise enough: a little premature in the two first instances; a little too indulgent in the third; not bold enough in the fourth; and aiming for an unattainable ideal in the last.

4 see Massignon, *La Mubāhala* (Paris, 1944), p 11

5 amongst others, Carlyle, Andrae, Barthélemy-St.-Hilaire, Goldziher, Massignon, Nöldeke, Turpin etc.

6 Renan, 'Mahomet', p 1080

7 Goldziher, *Dogme*, p 3

8 For at the same time, in reality, each one retains its own particular quality. Thus for instance the genealogies in the Bible, and the stories of ʿĀd and Thamūd in the Qur'an.

9 David, 'Analogies et Divergences entre les Légendes de la Bible et du Koran', in *Revue Sociologique et Historique*, 4th series, Vol 2, March-April 1884, p 125

10 In our choice of texts for this paragraph, we have taken care to avoid the double fault for which this exegetic method, known by the name of 'concordism', can so often be reproached: interpreting revealed texts in such a way as to put them in line with the results of science.

Zeal for explanation has pushed certain modern commentators of the Qur'an to demonstrate this 'concordist' tendency out of all proportion, to the extent of endangering the credibility of the faith itself. Sometimes they lack respect for the text, twisting it and forcing a meaning out of it which neither the vocabulary, nor the syntax, are giving to understand, and sometimes they have too much respect for the opinions of scholars, adopting even those hypotheses which are unverifiable or contradictory.

This double excess put aside, we not only find ourselves justified in comparing the givens of this instantaneous inspiration with the results of slow, methodical observation, but we judge it indispensable to the firmness of the faith. The Qur'an expressly invites us to discover its Divine source, on the one hand by meditating on it, and on the other by contemplating the signs which the Creator has left scattered in the world and in ourselves which bear clear witness to its absolute truthfulness:

> *Will they not then meditate on the Qur'ān? And if it were from any other than Allāh, they would have found in it many a discrepancy.*
>
> 4:82

> *We will soon show them Our signs in farthest regions and among their own people, until it is quite clear to them that it is the Truth …*
>
> 41:53

Now, in the examples cited here, it is not a question of interpreting, but of noting the striking identity between the pronunciations of the Qur'an, and scientific statements resulting from much prolonged research across the centuries, resulting in definite information thanks only to the collaboration of competent and specialized men, each in his own field.

Is this simple coincidence?

Is it possible that in the time of Ignorance a man unaided by any apparatus, left to his own natural enlightenment and limited observations could, on top of his basic moral, religious and social task, deal with matters of anatomy, meteorology, cosmology, animal and human psychology, and yet other branches of knowledge? All necessitating elaborated apparatus and collective experience complementing each other? And give us universal and eternal formulae on each subject, without leaving traces of error anywhere about his own era, environment or mentality?

11 It is not difficult to disengage the capital difference which, in many respects, distinguishes the facts announced by the Qur'an from facts treated by modern experimental psychology (telepathy, magnetism, spiritualism, psychometry, dreams, prevision, retrovision, etc.) and which, while proving the existence of something beyond the senses and the possibility of contact with a beyond, afford nothing certain about a Divine origin.

This difference resides first of all in how they perceive themselves. Not only do presentiments of distant events in scientific procedures suppose a voluntary and induced attitude, but the moment they arise within normal consciousness, they appear to have an uncertain character; they are possible, or probable. Every subjective assurance in this regard is certainly subject to easy falsification through the influence of some adverse suggestion (e.g. dreams or hypnotism).

The second difference is in their realization. Thus, for example, the American writer, Upton Sinclair, known for his methodical research on telepathy, affirms to us that of 290 experiments conducted by him and his wife, only 23 succeeded completely, and 53 partially [cited by al-ʿAkkād, *Allāh* (Cairo, 1947), p 38].

The final difference lies in their range: aiming towards an individual or a very limited period, human prevision has, in fact, a relatively mediocre field of application and never extends to eternal matters. In place of formulae of the most categorical nature, some repeat themselves, others depend on certain circumstances, and others soon find themselves invalid. In every case they are systematically and precisely confirmed.

But our own position here consists less in a demonstration in favour of the Qur'anic thesis, than in a refutation, by its absurdity, of the opposite thesis. If this revelation is nothing more than the product of an exalted imagination, we should have to be able to find at least one example in the Qur'an where a disparity between words and reality is manifested.

12 Lammens, *Berceau*, p 89

Index